THE ORIGINS OF FREE PEOPLES

THE ORIGINS OF FREE PEOPLES

JASON CARO

continuum

Continuum International Publishing Group
80 Maiden Lane, New York, NY 10038
The Tower Building, 11 York Road, London SE1 7NX

www.continuumbooks.com

© Jason Caro, 2011

ISBN-13: 978-1-4411-1304-7 (hardcover)

Library of Congress Cataloging-in-Publication Data
Caro, Jason, 1965–
The origins of free peoples / Jason Caro.
    p. cm.
Includes bibliographical references and index.
ISBN-13: 978-1-4411-1304-7 (hardcover : alk. paper)
ISBN-10: 1-4411-1304-5 (hardcover : alk. paper)
1. Liberty. I. Title.

JC585.C334 2011
320.01'1—dc22

                                                                    2010033719

Typeset by Newgen Imaging Systems Pvt Ltd, Chennai, India
Printed and bound in the United States of America

Father . . .

Contents

Acknowledgments

This project is the result of the convergence of many forces, or more euphemistically, many influences. What began as a search for a dissertation topic that would meet a number of parameters including practicality, duration, and interest for myself and for those wiser than me who would oversee it became, via many twists and turns, this book. It was inspired by the experience of the occupied, colonized, and displaced peoples and their valiant leaders who certainly have no need for this collection of researches. In a way, it is also an expression of appreciation for the free peoples among whom I have always lived. It is possible that the reason for the lateness of publication was the many challenges encountered along the way or that its message had to become somewhat more familiar than it was then.

This book began as the application of a particular way of thinking about politics as entirely productive, even of apparent mistakes or lapses. It is the synthesis of debates and thinking with others at a particularly fruitful time on the scintillating campus of UCLA. First and foremost I must thank Carole Pateman for being a great teacher of political theory. Her insight stunned me at the time and still does today. Along the way, there are a number of names that come to mind and were helpful in getting the project underway including Blair Campbell, Sam Weber, Richard Ashcraft, and Brian Walker. There are other teachers who I am sure contributed as well, albeit indirectly, from an intense period of graduate study undertaken at the University of Chicago.

I also owe thanks to those fellow learners who made the immediate intellectual environment at the time so rich with debates that forced deeper reflection in the face of controversy. A name that comes to mind in this regard is Dan O'Neill who insisted that critique was not enough. There are other names to recall as well—too many—including Rich Goldin, Denise Kimball, Rich Moushegian, and Shefali Jha. Those whom I have left out of this list are victims of my poor memory. But their help has been much appreciated.

I would be quite remiss if I did not thank profusely those staff people who made everything possible then such as Barbara Jess and Nancy Gusten. Also I wish to thank the staff of the various libraries that became, at times, my second home. The University Research Library staff at UCLA facilitated not just this project but my own learning process. Also not to be forgotten are the staff at the Coates Library who welcomed a stranger generously. Trinity University is clearly a beacon of what used to be called a liberal education.

The details of writing the manuscript were assisted by my editor, Marie-Claire Antoine, who also went beyond the call of duty in other respects helpful to this writer. Also supportive were the various reviewers who strengthened the work. A. Campbell made some sensible points to improve the structure. My mother, R. Salinas, was helpful in checking references. In any case, the errors that will doubtless be found in the following pages are entirely my fault. In keeping with a productive sense of the political, however, I console myself with the presumption that even they must bear some purpose.

Preface

Thankfully, problems of longstanding concern and import almost always have a reliable guide for consultation. For Thucydides the first problem of history was the political fate of free people. Himself an Athenian and a general, Thucydides thrust aside his own lifelong prejudices to discern what had gone wrong with the most successful free people of all time. His answer was that they had forgotten their origins or the careful processes needed to foster and maintain their liberty. Thucydides' recitation of Pericles' Funeral Oration "repeatedly conveys an image of the freedom of Athenian life."[1] But his history also suggests that the successes that arrived almost daily in their free life blinded them to the delicate arrangement that their politics absolutely required. So sure of the continued windfall of liberty, the ancient Athenians believed that it could also be spread relatively easily to the surrounding states and beyond. Hence Athens installed the world's first alliance of democracies, the Delian League, to support other free states. Thucydides was amazed that again and again the Athenians were misled by wrongheaded assessments of their origins until they finally drove their league and their state to destruction. He left his great book behind as a cautionary tale about the importance of being educated to the origins of free peoples.

What is worrisome is that, if anything, the political and philosophical consideration of free peoples today is at least as misinformed about their origins as were Pericles' confident Athenians. This effect is rather strange because, although the concept of the liberty of the people is limited to a relatively few blips on the radar screen of ancient or medieval political theory, it is a major topic of modern political thought. So there can be little excuse for such a lapse. Worse, if those who pride themselves on philosophical rigor and clarity of expression on political matters do not manifest enough awareness of the origins of free peoples, how much more awareness can be expected of others? Occasionally there are flashes of insight but usually not enough to avert disaster. The recent testimony of a senior general that the invasion and liberation of another country would be a costly matter requiring "several hundred thousand troops" and a lengthy stay showed precisely such insight into the origins of free peoples. Like the message from that other ancient general, it was a reminder that there is no such thing as "freedom on the cheap." The general's remarks were rejected by the politicians, and he was quickly cashiered from the service. And what came to be called Operation Iraqi Freedom was initiated with a much smaller, "nimbler" force than recommended and without the resources allocated for long-term reconstruction. The result was costly for millions of people displaced or killed by the experiment. That failure to enable a free people was not simply, as has been thought, because of cynical decision making or because "freedom's untidy" but due also to a stubborn lapse in the modern and contemporary political thought of freedom. This lapse in the political thought of freedom, like the fracture in the Liberty Bell, reappears repeatedly despite attempts to patch it.

The point is that there are two ways to consider the origins of free peoples, one expensive and one cheap, one unfamiliar and the other familiar. Or, since this claim is yet too big to sustain, the testimonies of Thucydides and Shinseki reveal that free peoples should have an alternative account of origins. As free peoples, plausible accounts of their origins provide the deepest bases for life plans, for policy proposals, and for decisions of peace and war. It is understandable that free peoples, and those political theorists who thoroughly expound upon their favorite value, would first seek the low-hanging fruit or take the easy and familiar route. But what the generals noted above suggest is that, at least under conditions of extremis, what is familiar is not necessarily advisable. Perhaps that old lesson in skepticism ought to be extended to every contemporary moment of free life.

There has been so much study of the free peoples that a great deal of political knowledge of their origins is available, but because of its context, such as when it was developed or how it was to be deployed, that knowledge can be misleading. For example, modern and contemporary political theory contends, even celebrates, that freedom is *latent*, "natural," a "self-evident truth," or "intuitive" to humankind (which is rather heroic in the face of historical evidence indicating that women and men have mostly been slaves).[2] Of course, at a time when the liberties of the people were said to be the gift of royalty, in some quarters of seventeenth-century England, for instance, it scores great ideological points to be able to counter that liberty is your birthright.

Latent liberty also lets free peoples believe that they have received something wonderful for nothing, perhaps because they were just that much smarter or that much more blessed than anyone else. And as with Thucydides' Athenians, since their freedom seems so obviously valuable, it is unthinkable that it will not be readily adopted by other peoples too. Hence the latter are considered not so much nonfree as yet to be free peoples leading recently to myopic policies that are supposed to release their latent liberty such as the "structural adjustment" of African economies or the promotion of entrepreneurship in rural India. According to Arendt, forgetting the political, indeed worldly, origins of liberty also leads to perverse foreign policy. Quite critically, Arendt notes, "her own failure to remember that a revolution gave birth to the United States and that the republic was brought into existence by no 'historical necessity' and no organic development but by a deliberate act: the foundation of freedom. Failure to remember is largely responsible for the intense fear of revolution in this country . . . with the result that American power and prestige were used and misused to support obsolete and corrupt political regimes that long since had become objects of hatred and contempt among their own citizens."[3]

The second cache of available knowledge regarding the origins of free peoples reveals that because they live in a morally imperfect world they must invariably come under *threat*. What can be called anti-freedom was a watershed event in their modern, revolutionary development, and it has been a likelihood ever since. For example, it was only after the death of Charles Stuart that the English revolutionaries celebrated their "first year of freedom."[4] The modern political theory of freedom is obsessed with anti-freedom, so much so that it might be more accurate to consider it the political theory of anti-freedom. There is practically a competition among the liberal thinkers as to who can come up with a new name for anti-freedom. Some examples, to be addressed in detail shortly, include incoherence (Swanton), immorality (Raz), irrationality (Benn), domination (Pettit), oppression (Mackinnon or Patterson), arbitrariness (Locke), absolutism (Lord Acton), and coercion (Berlin). The effects of this obsession are profound. From a psychological standpoint, to be born under threat and to live with it continuously would qualify as either the cruelest infliction of trauma or as paranoia. Ironically, the political reactions of such wary peoples become threats to others and include the tendency to regicide, to war, or even to seek out the coming threat preemptively.

However, it is *liberation*, not latent liberty and external threat, that is the main feature of the origins of free peoples. Liberation is the simplest, one-word term for the necessary practices that enable free peoples. Their freedom is not latent but the product of ongoing, expensive, and specialized practices. Every pupil trained to say the pledge of allegiance, every celebration of Independence Day, museum exhibits, parades, monuments, historians' lectures and books, and politicians' speeches are just a few examples of the productive, maintenance effort that is needed. The work of liberation also involves not only tackling or neutralizing external threats but threat production. Anti-freedom turns out to be a rather special attribute, for it is not a threat to ethnicity, to religious integrity, to party discipline, to the clan, or to anything else but free peoples. But an imperfect world cannot be expected to send along just such perfect threats all of the time. Rather they must be carefully refined, like ore into jewelry, until recognizable as anti-freedom. The tremendous expenditure of resources and disciplinary expertise needed in this regard range from carceral, prosecutorial, bureaucratic, criminological, and military to journalistic. The "world" or "humanity" is then confirmed as morally "imperfect" when every newscast begins with incidents of illegal, anti-free activity, and every other official act is devoted to the security of the homeland.

The account of origins offered in the following pages supplements, in crucial ways, what the *other* account does not communicate. Free peoples would not exist were they to actually wait for nature or self-evidence to supply them with liberty or for the morally imperfect world to supply them with perfect threats to freedom. In truth they have to take action, of a particular sort, for their freedom. In other words they have practical, traceable, ongoing, replicable origins. Even if these practices have been forgotten, or more likely, if they are called by some other name, they must still be underway. Since free peoples are defined by *high liberty* or by the adoption of freedom as their paramount political value (and not equality, fairness, happiness, or some combination equivalent), what has been forgotten of their origins is a political action. It brings advantages to them: that freedom is easy rather than hard, a blessing rather than a product entirely of political practices, and so, dear enough for revolution or war.

To recall the full origins of free peoples, then, is also a political act, which is advantageous too but for another, more skeptical, yet humane sort of free people. Liberal political theorists, as the traditional exponents of the politics of high liberty, are the obvious starting point to fully recall the origins of free peoples, but liberal politics may not be the end result of this recollection. Consider the question at the personal level. What would it mean to discover that you were using so much more energy and resources than you knew to live the life that you were leading? Would it be paralyzing, depressing, or perhaps inspiring? Would one nod to the discovery and forget again? Or does an additional account offer new resources to draw upon for debate and planning?[5] It is presumptuous to think that a writer can control the effect of his discourse, but this project began with the aim of sensitizing readers to the hidden, harsh aspects of liberation and with the wish of their amelioration. That modest motivation has not changed. It begins with a review of accounts of origins rooted in human nature and ends with an account rooted in ongoing political practices. It begins with the presumption of the progress of freedom for all peoples and ends with the disclosure of the startling fate of the free peoples themselves.

Notes

1. Connor, *Thucydides*, 123.
2. "Liberty being only an exemption from the dominion of another, the question ought not to be how a nation can come to be free but how a man comes to have dominion over it; for till the right of dominion be proved and justified, liberty subsists as arising from the nature and being of man," Sidney, *Discourses Concerning Government*, 510.
3. Arendt, *On Revolution*, 219.
4. "Whereas Charles Stuart, late king of England . . . hath by authority derived from parliament been and is hereby declared to be justly condemned, adjudged to die, and put to death for many treasons . . . And whereas it is and hath been found by experience that the office of a king in this nation and Ireland . . . is unnecessary, burdensome and dangerous to the liberty, safety and public interest of the people . . ." from *An Act for the abolishing the kingly office in England and Ireland, and the dominions thereunto belonging, 17 March 1649*; Kenyon, *The Stuart*, 306.
5. Ciaranelli, "The Circle of Origins," 137.

1

Introduction

The typical explanation for the origins of free peoples has been based upon the *usefulness* of freedom for them. For example, in his *Freedom in the History of the West*, Patterson argues that archetypal eras of liberty in the ancient Athenian and Roman republics only emerged after their eras of slavery.[1] What Patterson calls "personal liberty" was embodied first among those neediest of freedom, in particular among slaves and those women who faced slavery as a possibility. As evidence, Patterson refers to the Hellenistic writings of the slave Epictetus who spoke at length of his love of freedom. Patterson also points out how Homer's Andromache, the Trojan wife of Hector, expressed fear at her loss of personal liberty should she be enslaved by the Greeks.[2] For Patterson, the usefulness of freedom for slaves and for such women is clear enough. After all, there could be little that was attractive about slavery or "social death," as he defines the condition. Thus, "to the question of the origins of freedom. . . . There was the individualized domination of the slave by his captor, the slave's powerlessness, and his social death . . . Note, however, that the slave desperately desired his freedom. Throughout his years of enslavement he made frequent attempts to escape, the certainty of his eventual slaughter no doubt reinforcing this desire."[3] What Patterson suggests is that because of his terrible social condition the slave first understood the usefulness of freedom, which his captor, for whom personal liberty was less useful, does not and cannot know. (The master, it turns out, knows only of "sovereignal freedom," which has today become a defunct type according to Patterson). Once Patterson shows that slaves were the first to become aware of the usefulness of personal, individualized liberty, amply evidenced by their repeated efforts to escape, the emergence of a fully free society from a slave one becomes almost a technical question of the education of the "masters" to its value as well.

When the masters do not quickly enough recognize the usefulness of liberty, then strong methods have been deployed to remind them of it. Various examples of this transformation, beyond the familiar English, French, or American revolutions, include the celebrated interpretation of the Magna Carta as a case of forcing freedom from the powerful, the emancipatory efforts of abolitionists and the Northern States during the American Civil War, and, more theoretically, Kojeve's master–slave dialectic.[4] Such is also, for instance, the familiar logic of Mackinnon's massive *History of Modern Liberty*, which "traces" freedom as "political rights" from its "origins" in Europe's medieval era.[5] Although only roughly cognizant of their liberty, the "masses" thought well enough of it to resist their feudal lords in a series of rebellions, thereby beginning a "progressive," emancipatory movement that has since gained strength and legitimacy. On Mackinnon's reading, the revolts of downtrodden city dwellers and peasants from the Middle Ages onward occurred because freedom was perceived to be useful to their desperate concerns.

The usefulness thesis of origins, then, is that freedom is considered useful by those who have or seek it, and so it becomes reasonable for them to better secure it. But it should not be thought, as it too often is, that only the weak (e.g., Patterson), the wronged (e.g., Locke), or the downtrodden (e.g., Mackinnon) fit this model of origins. An entirely consistent twist on the usefulness model has been to extend it to powerful elites who also find it useful or in their interests for freedom to originate. For example, Barrington Moore's *Origins of Social Dictatorship and Democracy* is also a study of the origins of freedom. Moore states, "[a]s one begins the story of the transition from the preindustrial to the modern world by examining the first country to make the leap, one question comes to mind almost automatically. Why did the process of industrialization in England culminate in the establishment of a relatively free society?"[6] Moore's answer is that an "agricultural bourgeoisie" came to first require guaranteed economic and then political liberties because of their stake in a growing international trade in wool products. The feudal system of rights and fealty, which had long been a feature of English politics, came to be a threat to these burgeoning interests. Moore recounts how the agricultural bourgeoisie undermined the feudal system through the enclosure of wooded lands needed by the peasantry. They also supported the destruction of the monarchy in the English Civil War, thereby paving the way for the useful economic and political "rights" that are well known today.

Although not as familiar, applying the usefulness thesis to elites is still found to be a practical explanation for its origination. Today influential studies from international affairs suggest that it is neither slaves nor any other social underclass that initiates liberty but elites in a transitional process known as "liberalization." In *The Origins of Liberty*, a comparative politics study, the central question is when do elites find it useful to liberalize? Specifically, when "will sovereigns conclude that they can maximize their benefits or minimize costs by opening up spaces for their subjects to exercise political or economic freedoms."[7] The answer, again, is that liberty arises when elites find it useful or in their interests to permit it. In one version of this model, Rogowski suggests that an important factor in elite calculations for liberalization is fear of (human) "capital flight."[8] Particular groups in a society become especially important at certain critical moments. For example, periods of war or economic growth create a demand for the youth demographic and so elites will be motivated to extend the franchise at such times. The pressure to liberalize is especially compelling if valued groups can exercise an option to emigrate. The suggestion then is that it can become useful to extend political liberties, to have freedom originate so to speak, based upon elite calculations of their own interests.

But whether their liberty emerges because of its usefulness to elites or to nonelites, it always does so because of a *threat*. That has been the typical rationale and the spur for the origins of free peoples, if the many accounts are any indication. Why did freedom originate?—because that which is so useful, dear liberty, became threatened. Alternatively, why did the free emerge?—because their liberty became threatened. For over 300 years the central question for the free peoples has been, now that a threat has arisen, be it the "Redcoats," the "Communists," "masters," "criminals," "coercion," "cruelty," or "capital flight," what is to be done? The answer has been that freedom needs to more fully originate. Every effort to better secure a free people in this regard is designed to vanquish, or more pragmatically, to minimize the threat to their freedom (which is why such freedom has lent itself to calculations of optimality, maximization, equilibrium, or to "making the best of a bad job," as Benn put it)[9].

Contemporary philosophers are also concerned with showing how freedom is useful or in human "interests" and such utility is most definite when it is threatened. In contrast to the historians however, with their emphasis on a threatening personage or action, the philosophers of freedom are notable for anatomizing all possible restrictions upon liberty so as to show precisely how each one detracts from it, thereby permitting the clearest possible picture of freedom's usefulness. Their thoroughness of classification has even elicited some comment. Regarding one such philosopher, Christine Swanton, Kristjannson notes, "Swanton ends up

with a definition which is even more permissive than MacCallum's schema
. . . accepting as constraints on freedom all kinds of flaws, breakdowns, and
restrictions on practical activity that limit the potential of human beings
as agents."[10] Perhaps Swanton does end up with a broad conception but,
more importantly, it is one that is proven useful because her thorough
review of restrictions suggests each of the different ways that liberty is in
"human interests." For example Swanton explains that "executive failure,"
as a kind of akrasia, detracts from freedom because of the inability to put
one's commitments into action.[11] If the akratic could put a commitment to
seek employment into action (i.e., if his freedom were not constrained so),
then notice how useful it would be to this unemployed individual (and to
anyone else, of course). Swanton thus confirms one facet of the usefulness
of freedom (that a commitment can be acted upon) were it not constrained
by that particular flaw. Once her discussion expands to track the effect of
every type of constraint, each of the different ways that freedom can be
useful emerge as well. In other words, Swanton demonstrates how freedom
originates because of its usefulness, albeit with the philosophical goal
of "coherence." Another model from contemporary philosophy that makes
the same point is Benn's *A Theory of Freedom*. But in this case the various
threats to freedom or "autarchy" have an explicitly psychological cast
and range from schizophrenia to psychosis. If, to take one of Benn's
examples, the "catatonic" is unable to act because he so thinks of himself
as an "object" of the world, that "deficiency" in turn demonstrates the
usefulness of freedom for surely it is better to determine one's own fate.
There are a host of such threats cataloged by such philosophers and
each constraint allows them to reveal some useful aspect of freedom and
thereby enable freedom to more clearly emerge or originate. If the impact
of Swanton's executive failure or Benn's catatonia upon liberty seems
strange to the average citizen for whom fear, want, or tyranny would be
more important, it should be kept in mind that these philosophers aim at
having the usefulness of freedom thoroughly clarified by demonstrating
how it is useful in every conceivable way.

Of course, the best-known usefulness accounts of origins have come
from political theory. They are so famous that they overshadow perhaps
every study of noncommunitarian liberty whether or not they are cited
explicitly. Two accounts that are especially notable are Locke's *Two Treatises
of Government* and Jefferson's *Declaration of Independence*. Thomas
Jefferson's *Declaration* is a proclamation of the emergence of a free people
from beneath the shadow of tyranny.[12] With some eloquence, it lists the
offenses of King George III that led the American people to desire to break

away from Britain and advance their liberty more fully.[13] In the case of Locke, the usefulness of liberty becomes evident with "the state of war" where criminals threaten the property and lives of their fellows. It is a state of excess where both injurer and injured engage in an escalating cycle of violence against each other. So it is no wonder that Locke's individuals come together and agree—literally contract—to set up a civil society that will secure their life and property with guaranteed civil and political liberties.

The main problem with the usefulness account of origins is that it only testifies to the valuation of freedom, not to what absolutely must happen for it to originate. Such accounts are tautological, for they essentially repeat the point that freedom has long been valued by the free. They are also blindly partisan. Just because liberty is perceived as useful to those peoples who subscribe to it does not necessarily mean that such valuation has been a major factor in its origins. What it means to become free may have its own rules, irrespective of whether it is valued or desirable. If only such freedom could be approached neutrally, without the warm heart about its usefulness, a science of freedom, or an "eleutherology," could focus solely on what enables it instead of beginning with the view that freedom is considered useful and then reciting past manifestations of this valuation, beginning with the earliest intimations of this bias among slaves or elites. That free peoples like their freedom is a separate matter from its origins. We have so far heard a great deal about a causal relation between the valuation of freedom and its origins; it is now time to consider the role of freedom's imperatives.

Chronology

The linchpin of the usefulness account of the origins of free peoples is its distinctive chronology. There must be at least a fraction of the freedom that is to come already in place before its threat arises for the usefulness thesis to work. Otherwise there would be no way to recognize a threat as a threat to freedom and the typical rationale for the origins of this wary political life form could not arise. It is thus imperative that at least a bit of the freedom to come be already first or prior to its threat. To be free can then be the *status quo ante* that is later disrupted by its constraint or threat. Consider, for example, Locke's famous version of the account: "First I am in the state of nature, then I commit an injury, then I consciously refuse to make reparation and resort to force. That I am arguing is the logical ordering of Locke's thought."[14] For the usefulness thesis to work, there is no way around this sequence of postulates. Injury can be known as a threat to freedom only because of when it arises in the "logical ordering of Locke's thought." Whether what is injured is the freedom of one or many, such injury can only be determined when at least some freedom is already in place to be injured. Otherwise there would be no way to tell "injury" from a clan dispute, misfortune, hubris, or an act of the gods. Ashcraft therefore has to insist that freedom came "first" and "then" injury if the rationale for the origins of Lockean freedom is ever to hold sway.

But there is a further way to tell that at least some freedom and not anything else must come before its threat in the usefulness thesis of origins. Remaining with the familiar case of Locke for a moment, it turns out that the state of nature is not only the "first" state in Locke's famous account. It is also a state of pure or "perfect Freedom." For all free peoples—that is, for those peoples who certify freedom as their paramount value—in the beginning was freedom and only freedom. Locke noted, "[t]o understand Political Power right and derive it from its Original, we must consider what State all men are naturally in, and that is, a State of perfect Freedom to order their actions and dispose of their Possessions and Persons as they think fit."[15] The characterization of the natural state as one of perfect freedom has implications for the course of its development that cannot be avoided. Locke insisted on the excellent distinction that while it is a state of liberty, it is not a state of license. That is, Locke's "perfect freedom" has distinctive rules or parameters such as the right to individually dispose of possessions and the injunction that the individual does not have the right to suicide. Thus Locke notes that while the state of nature gives "great freedom" to order one's possessions and person, nevertheless the "state of nature has a Law of Nature to govern it . . . that no one ought to harm another in his Life, Health, Liberty, or Possessions."[16] To live in such a state means "to be free from any Superior Power on Earth, and not to be under the Will or Legislative Authority of Man, but to have only the Law of Nature for his rule."[17] Given these markers of natural liberty, should harm, injury, or any other deviation from the law of nature arise in the Lockean account, the state of nature must be transfigured into some other state. This other state, Locke insists, is properly called the "state of war." Hence, "here we have the plain difference between the State of Nature and the State of War, which however some men have confounded . . . Men living together according to reason, without a common Superior on Earth with Authority to judge between them, is properly the State of Nature. But force, or the declared design of force upon the Person of another, where there is no common Superior on Earth to appeal to for relief, is the State of War."[18]

Locke's insistence on this distinction is well taken. But let it not be too well taken lest it be forgotten that there is not only a substantive "plain differ-ence" between these states but a chronological one too for it can never be the initial state but only a subsequent or later one that contains injuries to freedom. It is the injurers in a subsequent state that spur the full emergence of Locke's free people. "To avoid this State of War . . . is one great reason of Men putting themselves into Society, and quitting the State of Nature."[19] As is often interpreted, Locke's individuals are so inconvenienced by the circumstances of the state of war that they contract into a civil order that will secure their liberties with limited political institutions.

The reason that Locke's individuals can advance their freedom when they are threatened is because they can look back to their state of nature and recall how useful their pure liberty was in comparison with their current circumstances. With the recollection of their prior freedom in the state of nature, whether as myth, intuition, or as their view of history, it is easy to rationate the "plain difference" between it and the state of war and decide for some practical advancement of liberty. Thus "[i]f Man in the State of Nature be so free, as has been said; If he be absolute Lord of his own Person and Possessions . . . why will he part with his Freedom? . . . To which 'tis obvious to Answer, that though in the State of Nature he hath such a right, yet the Enjoyment of it is very uncertain, and constantly exposed to the Invasion of others . . . This makes him willing to quit this Condition which, however free, is full of fears and continual dangers: And 'tis not without reason that seeks out and is willing to joyn in Society with others . . . for the mutual Preservation of their Lives, Liberties, and Estates."[20] The invasions, fears, and dangers encountered in the state of war make for a good reason, in looking back to the initial or "natural" state of liberty, to quit it and enter another one that better preserves what they value. Long before it became fashionable to be pragmatic, Locke's under-standing of the origins of free peoples also harbored no illusions. Threats or inconveniences arose in the state of nature (somehow) and so there is no point in retaining that idyllic beginning, however "perfect."[21] Lockean liberty therefore has to advance or to originate more fully. His individuals decide to band together and fully inaugurate their freedom in a political and civil form that many observers could still recognize today.

Of course, it is not just Lockean political theory, but every version of the usefulness thesis of origins has at least a bit of the freedom to come as already prior. This is because without its chronology such freedom could not become threatened, could not be recognized as the useful option, and could not (more fully) originate. Some of the initial instantiations of liberty are quite well known, such as the "rights of man and citizens" or the "self-evident" truth of the *Declaration of Independence* that Americans have the right to be politically free. Other examples, such as Raz's "liberal authority" or Benn's "natural personality" are perhaps less well known but just as crucial to the development of their accounts of liberty.[22] Swanton, for example, presents what she calls the "background theory of freedom."[23] It is her state of nature, or her initial, or basic, instantiation of liberty. Like Locke's initial instance, the status of the background theory is vague but not because the law of nature is hard for some to discern. Nor is it because the historical record is unclear on the origins of freedom's first instance. In this case the background theory is hazy because it is only a set of "intuitions" of liberty. Kept together or "collocated" in their "raw" form, they constitute one's first sense of freedom and its value for those who subscribe to it. When this initial instantiation of freedom is contrasted against its various "flaws," Swanton's initially hazy "freedom" then clearly emerges as in "our interests." Each flaw is like a ministate of war against liberty, prompting Swanton to look back on her background theory and more clearly draw forth some aspect of it that is beneficial to "human flourishing."

The familiar account of the origins of the people's liberty, then, is not exactly that it emerged because of its usefulness. Rather, their freedom was already known to be useful (this being a self-evident truth or a natural law inscribed on the human soul) and although it is not known precisely when or how that happened (because it is only a self-evident truth or a natural law inscribed on the human soul), freedom's usefulness is nevertheless confirmed because when it was threatened it was fought for. This familiar account is the Jeffersonian or the Lockean version of the usefulness thesis. The more detailed philosophers' version of the tale is that freedom is already known to be in our interests (this according to an intuition, a belief structure, or a collocation of intuitions), and although it is not known exactly when or how that came about (because it is only an intuition, a belief structure, or a collocation of intuitions), the usefulness of freedom nevertheless becomes clear, "coherent," or "consistent" when freedom is threatened and we can then better draw out its value for us.

Thus the precise usefulness thesis of origins is that freedom has always already originated as useful, and although not much is known about those origins, that it originates because of its usefulness is confirmed by the strong reactions when it becomes threatened. Of course, from what is known of human history or from what is often charged against human nature, it might tempting to argue that there was never a time or place when there was only freedom or the free, momentarily in existence initially in their pure if hazy forms to then be better secured upon being threatened. And indeed, a host of early, conservative critics such as Sir Robert Filmer, Mary Astell, and Edmund Burke made precisely that charge when they first came upon this novel account of naturally free peoples.[24] Nonetheless, history or no, documented or not, for the sake of free peoples it must have been so. And for the sake of their freedom today it must still be so. Indeed so important is this imperative that thinkers, writers, and institutions work around the clock in free societies, as they have for generations, to make it sure that it is so.

Given this imperative of its chronology, that some bit of itself must already be prior, it turns out that the famous liberty of the usefulness thesis always originates as more freedom than before. For example, prior to the famous revolutionary struggles for Locke's or Jefferson's freedom, there had to already be somewhat less of such freedom. This sequential requirement, *not its usefulness*, is what is imperative because free peoples would not be possible without it. As it has so far been known, the standard account of the origins of free peoples, in the terms of the usefulness thesis, is not enough. By itself it cannot and has not accounted for all that is required. Freedom, however beloved, does not and has not originated because it is useful. As Nietzsche once put it, "[h]owever well one has understood the *utility* of any physiological organ (or of a legal institution, a social custom, a political usage, a form in art or in a religious cult), this means nothing regarding its origin."[25] Certainly let it be conceded that there is liberty and there are free peoples. That is the starting point for analysis. But they do not originate in the way that many of their champions believe. Rather than because of its usefulness, at least one factor in the origins of their freedom is that a fraction of it must come prior. So how does this happen?

Synecdoche

No aspect of liberty simply pops up out of thin air, as if nature were always smiling upon its origins. And so is it too for the free peoples. They were not free naturally nor were their intuitions of freedom simply already around. Nothing is for free, not even freedom nor its first glimmer on the scene of early modern political thought. There are inescapable rules to every game and the freedom of the usefulness thesis is no exception. This is the kind of conclusion that Friedrich Schelling came to in a deceptively slight volume entitled *Philosophical Investigations into the Nature of Human Freedom*. When Schelling analysed the freedom of God, he anticipated the question of why the divine could not operate in some other way than what he, Schelling, had found. After all, he had just completed a study of no less than God's liberty. Should not anything be possible in that mighty scheme? Schelling's strict reply: that is what is "necessary" for *that* liberty. Attempt that freedom differently and that freedom will not be possible. The point was that just because God could do anything does not mean that even His type of liberty, of the precise kind and at the precise moment that Schelling had investigated it, would remain exactly the same.[26] Yes, God could alter it, and while it would again be God's freedom, it would nevertheless be different since it would not be exactly the one that Schelling had analyzed. Keeping Schelling's strict lesson in mind, what is imperative for the origins of *this* freedom (of the familiar, usefulness thesis) is not that it is useful but that it arises in the proper sequence. That is, at least one absolute requirement in this case is that a lesser bit of such freedom is set to become more of itself. The key to the origins of free peoples is to keep what Nietzsche called a "steely eye" on what is imperative instead of on the heartfelt idea that liberty is our friend and helps us (it is and it does but like so many these days one sometimes conducts background checks on one's companions).

The strict imperative of a prior fraction of the freedom to come is the reason why, even when it is dubbed a mere "intuition" or "conjecture," some such initial glimmer of liberty is put forth in every single document of its origins.[27] So stringent is this necessity that proponents of the usefulness thesis conform to it no matter how oddly. (That a historian would go so far as to find the first instances of the liberty of the ancient republics in the thoughts of their slaves surely requires some suspension of disbelief). In a study of origins, however, where everything about its subject is serious business, such postulations are recognized as important, even when they are empirically hazy or doubtful. Whether on the parchment of the great *Declaration of Independence,* in the thinking of a contemporary philosopher, or in a work of history, this particular mode of freedom requires what is necessary for it: a little bit of itself as already prior. There must be a smidgeon, an inkling, a mythos, a belief, or an intuition of the freedom that is to come so that what threatens it can be perceived and recorded as a threat to our freedom. Only then, if the familiar accounts and narratives are any indication, can this freedom, and those who fully subscribe to it, originate.

The first question of this study, then, is what are the origins of the liberty of the people and specifically how is what is imperative for it possible such as that lesser bit of itself that must arise in its chronology? The answer has been placed in the record innumerable times and need only be reiterated: it is *posited* that there was already some useful freedom beforehand although not much is known of how it came about. When Jefferson says that the liberty of his Americans is a "self-evident" truth, or when Locke gestures to a "state of nature," or when Swanton thinks of a "background theory of freedom," or when this is rewritten and re-read in the pages of this book, what is being posited is precisely an underformulated, earlier version of the liberty to come—just what the doctor ordered to fill this freedom's chronological prescription. Precisely such production can therefore be counted as a specific, replicable, and necessary liberation practice since without it, this freedom and those that subscribe to it as their paramount value could not originate.

Such production is not as strange as it might at first sound for it suggests only that here is a mode or style of political life that requires a particular historiography. In differing ways, political societies the world over work hard to get their histories "right" and to keep them that way.[28] In South Africa, evidence that there was a thriving culture in precolonial times that included advanced goldsmithing, languished for decades in the basement of a university in Pretoria. Presumably the Dutch immigrants to southern Africa wanted to be able to prove that they had brought civilization first to the region.[29] The point is not that historical truth is "merely" a construct so much as that the production of history, its historiography, has important political effects. As Pocock put it, "the structure of the present is still thought to be vitally affected by the reconstruction which is made of the past. In such a period the writing of history is inevitably partisan, but it may not be worse for wear from that."[30]

In this case of getting the history right, it is by positing exactly what is imperative that freedom is enabled. But this action cannot be just any kind of postulation because the freedom involved is not just any kind of freedom. It is only that type said so many times to originate because of its usefulness to free peoples. So the origins of such particular freedom will also be particular. And what must be posited in this case is a smidgeon of the freedom before that which is to come. Such fractional liberty is best distinguished as *proto-freedom* since this term bears the potential or quality of anticipating more of itself in the "future." By quality of anticipating more of itself I mean that proto-freedom comes to be better conceptualized or secured than it was "before" in the standard usefulness thesis of origins. This chronology can be traced in the second of Locke's famous *Two Treatises* with the transition from the state of nature to civil society and beyond. But it can also be found in the transition from Swanton's background theory to coherent freedom, or from Jefferson's self-evident truth of American freedom to fully fledged, secured civil and political liberties.

To ever wind up as more of itself, however, proto-freedom has to be, like Goldilock's porridge, just right. Too much of it, too well conceptualized, and freedom will have already originated in full. On the other hand, if there is too little proto-freedom, then it could not come under threat and thereby require its development or advancement in response. Thus, for proto-freedom to be capable of advancement, it has to be both clear *and* unclear. It has to be prior and also be unclear how it came to be prior. Precisely such ambivalence has been imperative for this freedom's origins. This requirement explains why there has been such a lackadaisical attitude about the formulations of such earliest freedom even from philosophers like Swanton or Benn who make strong claims to coherence and consistency. Proto-freedom has ranged in form from popular intuitions (Swanton) to philosophers' intuitions (Raz), self-evident truths (Jefferson), the natural state (Locke) to the thoughts of slaves (Patterson). These authors deployed proto-freedom every time not because the "analysis simply has to start somewhere" but because their mode of freedom would not be possible without it. In the next chapters I shall demonstrate the imperative of this requirement by asking that we try to imagine the emergence of the free peoples without presuming their proto-freedom, their states of nature, their *a priori* freedom, or the intuitions of their full liberty. It will quickly become evident that the freedom effect that they now know and enjoy would not be possible without proto-freedom and the practice that posits it.

In terms of what is imperative, the ambivalent conceptualizations of proto-freedom found with Locke, Jefferson, Swanton, Benn, and other commentators are not mistakes. They are also not guesses. And they are not signals that limits have been reached in the cognitive abilities of these authors. Nor do they reflect a gap in the available historical record regarding the formation of the people's liberty. Rather, proto-freedom must be precisely imprecise or underformulated for the full emergence of a free people to be possible. Not surprisingly, therefore, the right practice is needed to posit their proto-freedom just right. Such a practice comes under the heading of what ancient rhetoricians called synecdoche [*sunekdochê*], "the understanding of one thing with another" through "the use of the part for the whole."[31] Some ancient examples are, "*alopex*, fox skin for fox; *chelone*, tortoise shell for tortoise; *porphura*, purple dye for purple fish; *elephas*, ivory for elephant; *melissa*, honey for bee." How about proto-freedom for freedom? Part of freedom, a bit or smidgeon of it, being pronounced as prior and lesser, enables the rest—a part makes possible the whole. Who could imagine that intimation could do so much?

Of course, proto-freedom here also means the protofree, just as freedom should imply the free, for they do take their freedom to heart. This book of origins is as much a study of free bodies and minds as it is about their writings or treatises since it is only a study in the practices of a particular mode of free life. It does not matter so much in what format that freedom happens as that *that* freedom happens. The genitive case is deliberate here. This freedom has its own rules, which are distinct from those of power, reason, or history. That which is freedom may develop in a theory or in a history text or "out there" in the "real world" of political institutions and living beings. The old distinction between theory and practice does not hold when it comes to what is imperative for freedom. This is because what matters in terms of origins is not the format but simply how this specific mode of free life must originate. It is interesting, for example, that American liberty is always celebrated on the day that John Hancock flamboyantly signed a parchment and not, as might be expected from a realist interpreter, on that fateful day at Yorktown when Lord Cornwallis surrendered. Oddly enough, no one remembers that day when "the facts on the ground" were actually decided (sometime in October I think). Rather, the importance of liberty is reiterated always only on the day that it was "merely" declared or when a mere piece of paper was penned. The point is that freedom is a function of its own particular imperatives. The "self-evident" truth of Jefferson's American liberty may be the most unreal and unsupported of conceptions ever. Or it may actually inhere in every American ever born. When concerned solely with origins, no position has to be taken either way. The importance of Jefferson's claim and others like it come only from its crucial role as proto-freedom.

Indictment

Other than proto-freedom, there is one other effect that is imperative for free peoples. But it is immediately less benign and much more controversial. It is the production and refinement of what threatens the free, a threat that is here called *anti-freedom*. This term has been used before, in the work of Brown certainly and perhaps elsewhere.[32] Anti-freedom means that which is against freedom and which, by being so, depends for its existence upon that which it is against. The term anti-freedom thus stands as a reminder of the ongoing relation between freedom and that which is against it. This relation is recalled not because of some penchant for paradox but simply because anti-freedom has been imperative for the origins of free peoples. After all, in any testimonial of their origins, whether in the expositions of Swanton, Benn, Locke, or Jefferson, it is some form of anti-freedom that spurs the drive for the full advancement of their freedom. Indeed, there has been no modern discussion of noncommunitarian freedom, which has not also included a discussion of the threat to such freedom. This is not to say, brutishly, that anti-freedom is everywhere the same, as though Swanton's subtle "executive failure" is the same as Ashcraft's "injury" or Berlin's "coercion." No, what is the same is the effect of anti-freedom in the origins of free peoples, namely, as the spur for the full emergence of their liberty.

Like proto-freedom, anti-freedom has to be modulated just right for a free people to fully originate. If the threat to their freedom were too great, or if the problem of anti-freedom were too widespread, then the cause of liberty is lost and a different priority, perhaps survival or collaboration will be the order of the day. (Is this logic not ultimately why the mind-boggling threat of nuclear annihilation and mutually assured destruction had to be defused?) On the other hand, if the threat to freedom is too faint or insignificant, then there would be no need for more of it to originate and the free might today still inhabit their foundational Edens such as Algernon Sidney's or John Locke's states of nature. Anti-freedom therefore has to be present or around as a threat but not overly so. That is, like proto-freedom, anti-freedom has a very special modulation or valence. The catch is that nothing so carefully modulated simply pops up out of thin air, whether in philosophy, society, or nature, and certainly not again and again over a span of centuries. Quite specific techniques, institutions, practices, ways of thinking, or to put it more simply, origins must be continuously brought to bear for it.

Does all of the discussion of production and effect here mean that threats to freedom do not really exist? Is it not obvious that such threats exist now, have existed, and have the potential to do so again in the future? Have not innumerable accounts of American or English history, as well as those of other free peoples, noted precisely such threats? Alternatively, does not an individual, as he walks nervously through a darkened alley, perceive a threat to his freedom? It turns out that the related but more fundamental question is how is it possible to claim that such threats are threats to freedom? My response to this latter question has already been given. It is only because of a peculiar and definitive chronology that such threats are obvious. That is, it is only because their freedom is considered to have come first or to have been prior already, be it naturally, historically, or intuitively that threats to the free can then be identified as such.

What should be obvious to free peoples is not the empirical existence of threats in history, in the world, or in their neighborhoods, but their unusual specificity, for they are not just any kind of threat but threats to freedom (i.e., anti-freedom). They are not, for example, threats to clan, to religious orthodoxy, to ethnolinguistic cohesion, or to the official political party. They are also not threats by chance (nowadays called acts of God by the insurance companies). Indeed, that threats to the free are so obvious today should be taken not as the dazzling confirmation that they exist but rather that a tremendous amount of specialized ideological work, conducted at the immense scale of a society, enables such threats to be so readily "obvious" as threats to the free.

Unfortunately and fortunately it does seem that threats to the free often arise in just the right amount and valence. Typically this is said to happen because the very "world" is imperfect, which is to say it is not totally threatening but somewhat so. As Gray notes, "we do not live in a world in which there can be no impediments."[33] Or as Thomas Paine put it in *Commonsense*, "[h]ere then is the origin and rise of government, namely, a mode rendered necessary by the inability of moral virtue to govern the world; here too is the design and end of government, viz., freedom and security."[34] The typical view of the source of threats to freedom is that they are simply a function of the imperfection of the "world." That is, while it has some freedom in it, it also has some threats too; it is imperfect. And who could deny it? One hears the complaint often enough. "Today, liberty faces a number of threats, new instruments in the age-old effort by its enemies to destroy its exercise."[35] It is probably not too far-fetched to claim that every political strategy in human history has had its opponents. But what has been stumbled upon here is a strategy, indeed a way of political life, that so requires "threats" for its operation that they are cast as a function of the very world.

What is suspicious about the imperfection of the world in the discourse of free peoples is that such imperfection does not have to be explained; it is part of the world after all. This "obvious" fact fits quite neatly with the usefulness thesis of origins because what matters most in that regard is not how the threat arose but what is to be done about it. With the very world imperfect, the origins of any particular threat, from Benn's psychotic, to Ashcraft's injurer, to the latest perpetrator featured on the evening news, do not have to be explained. To be sure, such threats need to be worried about and managed. And it would go a long way in dealing with such threats if their causes were better understood (hence the 200-year-old effort of criminology to do just that). But that much understanding is ultimately unnecessary because the priority is not so much its cause but that the threat is "out there" and needs to be countered. For instance,

> [s]ome of these relationships [of domination] will have originated historically in consent, while others will not. But it is important to notice that that is not to the point under our account of domination. Whether a relationship sprang originally from contract or not, whether or not it was consensual in origin, the fact that it gives one party the effective capacity to interfere more or less arbitrarily in some of the other's choices means that the one person dominates or subjugates the other. . . . historical context is more or less irrelevant to whether domination occurs in a relation.[36]

The question of the cause of what Pettit calls domination, much less the freedom it threatens, is not what matters. What is pressing is that the threat is at hand. Thus,

> [t]he question as to whether . . . conditions [of domination] obtain is going to be salient for nearly everyone involved, since it is of pressing interest for human beings to know how far they fall under the power of others. And the fact that the conditions obtain, if they do obtain, is usually going to be salient for most of the people involved, since the kinds of resources in virtue of which one person has power over another tend . . . to be prominent and detectable. There is a salient question, then, and a salient basis for answering the question.[37]

The "salient question" in this example is what is to be done about anti-freedom, not where did it come from, nor how is it so. Indeed, the two latter questions of origins do not readily arise because (1) the problem of threat is simply a function of our imperfect world, and (2) the problem is pressing or "salient" enough that our theoretical, societal, and practical energies should be focused on defending against it. The fact that threats are in the world makes it foolish to ask about their origins. The fact that liberty is in jeopardy due to these threats makes such inquiry a dangerous distraction. This blind trust in the "facts" is why Nancy lamented that, "[u]nder these conditions, the philosopher wonders if he can do anything other than 'speak of freedom.'"[38]

The key to the origins of free peoples however is to remain focused on what is imperative for them. The pervasive notion of an imperfect world (not to mention an imperfect humanity) provides a clue because evidently what is necessary is that anti-freedom be a problem *and* that it not have clear beginnings (i.e., that the threat of anti-freedom is simply "out there").[39] This ambivalence about sources is advantageous because if anti-freedom had well-understood origins, if it was not just a dumb fact or an obvious function of an imperfect world, then it would be conceivable to go ahead and fix it once and for all. And if the problem could be solved once and for all, that would make securing freedom less of a priority (which suggests why the field of criminology, which has identified innumerable types of threats, has so far "failed" to find the "cause" of a single one[40]). However, when the origins of anti-freedom are hazy and that threat is pressing, then the task at hand must be securing the (already-present) liberty of the people. Like today's random or senseless terrorist act, anti-freedom functions most precisely as a threat to the free when its causes are kept obscure.

Again therefore what is needed for free peoples must be just right and the practice that fashions anti-freedom so accurately is called *indictment*. Ironically, indictment is a constructive technique that takes the form of charging "*this* is a problem for freedom" or "*that* is a threat to free people." This simple gesture, in political speech, in philosophical writing, or in the juridical setting when freedom is at stake is enough to implicate a threat to freedom. Interestingly, the ancient rhetoricians' term for accusation, *kategoro*, translates literally as "to assemble into position." Aeschines (1. 178) notes, "you allow the defendants to bring counter accusations against the complainants" [*eate gar tous apologoumenous antikatêgorein tôn kategorounon*]. What is instructive about the rhetorical deployment is its strategic emphasis. It bears no modern sense of the veracity or falsity of the accusation. The focus is upon the act of accusing or making a charge.

Of course, it is important both ethically and morally that no one should ever be falsely accused. This point cannot be stressed enough. Calumny has, at least since the time of Xenophon, correctly been considered one of the most awful practices. Every possible safeguard should be erected against it. However, with a steely eye trained on what is here imperative it must not be forgotten that all that is needed for freedom to originate is anti-freedom. It does not have to be true, false, guilty, or innocent. It may or may not also be granted those attributes but it ultimately only has to be anti-free (in the precise valence noted above) in order for the liberty of the people to advance more fully. This is because the practices that are involved in the production of their freedom have no ethical or moral obligations but only, shall we say, freedom obligations (i.e., "obligations" solely to what is necessary for this type of political life to originate).[41] This strictly possessive obligation is the reason why so many events that seem of dubious moral worth can still be framed in the name of liberty. For example, that freedom has been recognized even in instances of colonialism is because it has rules of its own that unfortunately are not the rules of ethics.[42]

The truth then does not make free, but what is imperative does, in this case being the effect of anti-freedom. Anti-freedom needs to be "out there" but in a special way. It must be threatening and without a clear idea of how it came about. Precisely this ambivalent formulation is what is imperative and is why anti-freedom is always the effect of an accusatory practice. "He threatens freedom!" is the basic gesture of indictment. "Executive failure," "harm," "domination," "catatonia," "injury;" the name-calling and finger-pointing has been endless in the discourse but also quite necessary. As Connolly has noted, "[w]e do not, for example, always use the word 'constraint' in our everyday discourse about obstacles to freedom. We speak variously of people being confined, deprived, restrained, oppressed, repressed, dominated, and coerced."[43] High liberty and the liberal thought of political freedom has long entailed such denunciation and must continue to do so. The practice of indictment has changed relatively little in three hundred years, although it has been refined. In a forthcoming section, readers can witness in grinding detail the process of indictment and the production of anti-freedom. Where Locke was content to identify only arbitrary kingship as threatening, a contemporary philosopher has recently identified over sixteen different types of "flaws" of freedom in a single monograph.[44]

One could well characterize the intellectual history of free peoples over the past three centuries not as the progressive expansion of liberty but as the renaming of threats to them. The free are necessarily obsessed and fascinated with threats because they could not exist without them. This is why, when contemporary philosophers so carefully categorize such threats, their pronouncements should be read as indicators of the threats that freedom needs in order to originate. They charge that this is a "flaw" of freedom or that is a "deficiency" of freedom. There is an analogous repetition of charges with the emergence of the anti-free today, first on the part of the police, then again with the prosecutor, then again with a court psychiatrist or other witnesses, then again with the jury, and again with the judge and the charge is repeated still again each day in his prison cell and beyond with parole hearings. Indeed, the execution of the "convict," after a slew of failed appeals, constitutes perhaps the most definitive act of indictment, of categorizing the anti-free (is this perhaps why public references to executed criminals always include their middle name?). Indictment is thus no trick of language or rhetoric for such accusation can also be written on the human body, not with a scarlet letter perhaps but practically nonetheless through the kinds of postures and confinements a body is held in. Strictly in terms of their origins, the difference between the free and the anti-free is not the moral difference between good and bad. It is rather the empirical and practical difference between being carefully unmarked and being carefully marked. Both marking gestures must be continuously employed for a free people.

It will undoubtedly be asked how is it that contemporary philosophers, politicians, the courts, and even an entire society can be said to be producing threats to the free rather than simply arresting, certifying, and punishing them? The response to this sincere question has been given. To be able to identify or classify the special category of anti-freedom requires the peculiar chronology that some liberty was already around as the *status quo ante* and so was prior to what comes to threaten it. Otherwise threats to the free could not be recorded nor identified as such. Perhaps the most controversial aspect of this book is that the crucial requirements of proto-freedom and anti-freedom are presented entirely as functions of human action. The initial condition of being free cannot simply have already been in place, as if conjured up by some secret magic. Rather, in the best tradition of social science, every aspect of freedom, of the free, and of being free becomes a matter of replicable and identifiable societal practices. So when a synecdoche projects some bit of freedom as prior, whether as "natural" or as "intuitive," that only means that a particular, and quite human, practice has been employed for that effect. Similarly, if indictment is repeated in order to set forth anti-freedom, that too only means that some practice has been deployed to that effect. If such practices, when replicated, enable a particular style of freedom or a special mode of free life, then such freedom and such free people can well be considered to be a function of identifiable, replicable, human actions. This kind of steely focus upon human practices at any and all times is how free societies can be characterized as simultaneously constructing and obfuscating both their past and their enemies. These are the main functions of free societies not shopping, nor entertainment, nor even capitalism. Free peoples know they were free to begin with but not how that started. And they know that they are threatened but not why. Ironically, this ambivalent understanding is the effect of their own origins.

Together, then, two practices make up the imperative origins of free peoples. Specifically, they are synecdoche and indictment producing the effects of proto-freedom and anti-freedom respectively. Who today has not heard the claim that the people are already free, say, as rights bearers, whether by nature, as according to common sense, or as a self-evident truth?

Such synecdoches can be discerned in innumerable history books and treatises, in celebrated declarations, pedagogies, or national anthems and are recycled in school and academic lessons. Indictment is also deployed in the same teachings, books, and declarations of liberty and is especially concentrated in the criminal court and prison systems of countries dedicated to high liberty. One should also not fail to take note of the media in this regard, for they seem to take special delight in pointing out far and near threats in the world. Free peoples are possible only via the repetition of these two practices and their effects, which take place on a vast scale using innumerable means and formats both theoretical and physical. The energy and effort involved in the origins of free peoples is enormous and specialized and is why their freedom modality might be considered as something of an extraneous value for other peoples without the commitment or the resources to expend in its service.

In contrast, then, to those other origins (i.e., as according to the usefulness thesis), the imperative origins do not resemble the uplifting and heroic accounts of revolutionary or other uprisings that are often associated with the emergence of free peoples. Rather, it means the ongoing reproduction of two required effects and this configuration of forces must be evident whenever freedom originates anew. What happened on July 4, 1776, and what happens on July 4 over two centuries later is procedurally equivalent because the *freedom to not be threatened* always has the same requirements. Every day is Independence Day because every day of such independence requires its origins. Just as it began, so must it continue, for so long as free society is affirmed, then the threat posed by a George III must be found. As Brown puts it, "[i]deals of freedom ordinarily emerge to vanquish their imagined, immediate, enemies, but in this move they frequently recycle and reinstate rather than transform the terms of domination that generated them."[45]

What might this political study of liberation mean in contemporary circumstances? For one thing, the formula and the cost of promoting liberty abroad, which has been a stated foreign policy objective of free states from ancient Athens to modern America, changes dramatically. Such promotion requires the generation of histories, paeans, museums, and treatises to install the history of a people as already free (and so also an educated class that will write of such primal liberty). So if Operation Iraqi Freedom was to be a genuine effort, Iraq's museums, schools, and colleges needed protection and reorganization before its oil and defense ministries.[46] The promotion of freedom also requires institutions that identify and manage threats to the free (rather than threats to the clan, to the family, to the ethnic group, or to the official party) since to be free requires the quite careful refinement of those who are anti-free. Thus it is the police and courts, not the army, that first need reorganization in any attempt to liberate others. Given such dramatic changes, it is perhaps not surprising that there has been resistance to incorporating this model (to the consternation of its promoters).

How Did This Study Originate?

A couple of nagging incongruities in the history of the free peoples led to the researches of this study. These incongruities raised questions about the history of the free peoples because, despite many claims to the contrary, it is not self-evident that their freedom was the same—that is, useful in the past. For one thing, the etymology of freedom does not suggest the sense of something that is useful. It is rather just the opposite. Freedom seems to be something of a luxury item. The etymological suggestion is always this: freedom does not arise with those who most desired or needed it such as slaves in bondage or women about to be captured in war. It did not come about through any self-interested, rational acts on their part, but came always from the very others who would find liberty least useful (e.g., not from Patterson's "slaves" nor his Greek/Roman "women," but from the "masters").

Etymologically, both liberty and freedom have very little to do with usefulness and interests.[47] Freedom is too warm for that as it comes from the Sanskrit word for one "dear" or "friend" and the Gothic *frijon* meaning love.[48] "Liberty" calls forth the quality of those who favor others or who have favorites and shower them with gifts. The trail was more obscured here, coming first from the Attic *eleutheria* and then through the Latin *liberalis*. In the Greek case, to be freed from a threat, such as the invasion of Xerxes, was a being made free, often in a "glorious" military fashion that would live on eternally. Such freedom was typically thanks to someone else not in need of it, such as the gods or good fortune. In the Latin to be liberal meant to give without restraint, almost the opposite of what it means to act rationally (and it still retains that connotation as in to spread a salve liberally).[49] Thus in the Roman context *liberalis* had the aristocratic sense of one who gives freely of oneself or is "frank."[50]

The second incongruity in the history of free peoples was that what came prior was not the same as what was to come because the prior liberty in their history had nothing to do with its usefulness. Freedom in the West began as a *gift* of aristocrats and royalty. "Liberty," said De Maistre, "has always been the gift of kings."[51] The freedom before the Glorious Revolution, and before Locke's "early modern" liberty, was not so much like that of the state of nature (i.e., a rational freedom that each bearer employs for profit), but was rather a quite dissimilar type that emerged from royal generosity. In the very spot where Locke saw opposition to liberty, namely, in Sir Robert Filmer's divine-right politics, was a well-developed, well-distributed style of liberty, granted by the king upon the petitions of his subjects. And in the freedom before the American Revolution, there was nothing self-evident about an American liberty that was useful and true for all men. Rather, according to the American Loyalists, all such "liberties" were a grant from the English sovereign and sustained by that extraordinary will. After all, the legal evidence was clear that every colony, and the liberties they had, were only the product of a royal charter or grant. On the Loyalist reading, the Patriots were destroyers of the laws and liberty who pursued blasphemous policies for selfish ends. Finally, in the freedom before the French Revolution, there was nothing akin to any inborn "rights of man," but there was an ancient style of liberty applied by that most innocent and generous of princes, Louis XVI, who was only too ready to give liberty to his subjects at their request.[52]

So what is the payoff of challenging the standard history of free peoples?—only the right, dare I say the liberty, to ask one question. If the freedom before that of today was *dissimilar*, and it will be seen that pre-revolutionary freedom was different indeed, why has it instead wound up as similar in the history and political theory books? A preliminary response: because some similar liberty as prior is imperative for the free peoples of today and so it is produced that way. As indicated at the outset, the point of this study is to recall the origins of free peoples. The dissimilar history of free peoples helps break the profound hold that the other account of origins has had upon so many contemporaries, a hold that leads too many to think that beloved liberty is simply lying about to be released abroad or defended at home. Typically that sequence of freedom's advance starts with a fraction of the same type of liberty (such as intuitions, a state of nature, or the notion of personal liberty in the mind of a slave) that then became threatened. More of the same freedom as was before, in the form of institutionalized civil and political liberties, is then the familiar practical response and progression.

But if the freedom beforehand was dissimilar, then the origins of the freedom of the state of nature or a type like it become a question. And that is the first task of this book: to raise the question of origins. This introductory chapter mirrors, in a concentrated fashion, the plan of the whole book.

I have suggested why this study of origins will begin with, of all things, pre-revolutionary liberty as royal grant. In terms of English history, the timing is not that far off the mark—Filmer wrote of liberty well before Locke and the latter's celebrated Glorious Revolution. Mary Astell, another monarchist thinker, also referred to the earlier mode of liberty as a royal grant and as utterly dependent upon that noble source. So the dissimilar history of liberty to be presented in Chapter 2 is not an implausible interpretation of what came before say, the English or the Glorious Revolutions (the latter especially is often associated with the full-scale emergence or the political "settlement" of a free people).

Importantly, by Chapter 3, the dissimilar history of liberty must be wiped out. Locke's *First Treatise* was a necessary prelude to the origins of the free peoples. Such work was necessary because their freedom advances or progresses from less to more of itself, say, from its hazy, natural state to guaranteed liberties in a liberal democracy. That could not happen if the liberty beforehand must originate by royal grant. Not surprisingly in the *First Treatise*, Locke completely erases such chronologically wrong freedom. Criticizing only Filmer's scriptural foundation for political power, Locke never mentions Filmer's conceptualization of liberty as grant. Locke nonetheless dismisses it into utter oblivion precisely by undermining its foundation. After Locke's *First Treatise*, his free peoples are then possible. No longer encumbered by the wrong history and freedom of Filmer and his ilk, Locke in the *Second Treatise* embarked on the project by postulating his "state of nature" (i.e., by a synecdoche). And he identified the "noxious" enemy of this free people through indictment. By Chapter 4 there is no need to go through so much trouble to draw out those productive practices. Another wrong, dissimilar history need not be postulated in order to provoke disclosure of the origins of free peoples. Instead some newer philosophers of freedom from the Rawlsian tradition are addressed directly in the performative terms of their own enabling efforts. In Chapter 5 I draw together the precise details of the origins of free peoples. Finally in the last chapter I attempt some remarks about the fate of free peoples as they continue to produce their hazy past and their threatening present in the new circumstances of globalization.

Notes

1. Patterson, *Freedom*, 17.

2. "When the average woman of sixth- and even fifth-century Greece paused to reflect on her condition, her musings must have run along the lines

of 'There but for the grace of the gods go I.' By empathizing with the slave end of the master–slave relation, then, women became more conscious of freedom," Patterson, *Freedom*, 78.

3. Patterson, *Freedom*, 16.

4. "[H]e will not cease to be Slave as long as he is not ready to risk his life in a *Fight* against the Master, as long as he does not accept the idea of his *death*. A liberation without a bloody fight, therefore, is metaphysically impossible," Kojeve, *Introduction*, 56. Also see Caro, "Looking," 916.

5. Mackinnon, *A History*.

6. Moore, *Origins*, 3.

7. Drake and McCubbins, *The Origins*, 5.

8. Rogowski, *Democracy*, 48.

9. Benn, *A Theory*, 59, 63.

10. Kristjansson, "Social Freedom," 179.

11. Swanton, *Freedom*.

12. Perry, *Sources*.

13. "All the indictments of George III's personal role and actions, which introduce the claim that his authority over the colonies is dissolved by reason of his misgovernment, serve to introduce the Declaration's chief verbal performance, which is a declaration of war, in the name of the American 'people,' upon the 'people' and 'state' of Great Britain. The proposition that all men are created equal introduces one people's right and power to declare itself independent of and at war with another. The Declaration is not a wholly benign document," from Pocock, "The American Founding," 58–59.

14. Ashcraft, *Locke's Two Treatises*, 205.

15. Locke, *Two Treatises*, II, §4.

16. Ibid., §6.

17. Ibid., §22.

18. Ibid., §19.

19. Ibid., §21.

20. Ibid., §123.

21. Thus, "for want of positive Laws, and judges with Authority to appeal to, the State of War, once begun, continues," Locke, *Two Treatises*, II, §20.

22. Raz, *Morality*; Benn, *A Theory*.

23. Swanton, *Freedom*, 30.

24. "[I]nalienable political rights of all men by virtue of birth would have appeared to all ages prior to our own as they appeared to Burke—a contradiction in terms," Arendt, *On Revolution*, 39.

25. Nietzsche, *Basic Writings*, 513.

26. Schelling, *Philosophical Investigations*, 84.

27. Simmons, *On the Edge*.

28. Nietzsche, *Untimely Meditations*.

29. Van Eeden, "The Colonial Gaze," 27.

30. Pocock, *The Ancient Constitution*, 245.

31. Smyth, *Greek Grammar*, §3047.

32. Brown, *States of Injury*, 41.

33. Gray, *Freedom*, 21.

34. Paine, *Political Writings*, 5.

35. Fowler and Orenstein, *Contemporary Issues*, 74.

36. Pettit, "Freedom as Anti-Power," 585.

37. Pettit, "Freedom as Anti-Power," 582.

38. Nancy, *Experience*, 2.

39. "The human mind reaches out to make intelligent use of the *noumenon*, the 'raw stuff out there,'" Benn, *A Theory*, 28.

40. "The intellectual reputation of discussions about the causes of violence is abysmal. Merely to announce causation as a topic of discussion will provoke the derisive groans of sophisticated scholars in the United States," from Zimring and Hawkins, *Crime Is not the Problem*, 111.

41. Nancy, *Experience*, 29.

42. Almost a century before Operation Iraqi Freedom, British General Maude declared in Baghdad, "our armies do not come into your cities and lands as conquerors or enemies but as liberators," Prasch, "Neoliberalism and Empire," 283.

43. Connolly, *The Terms*, 173.

44. See Swanton, *Freedom*.

45. Brown, *States of Injury*, 7.

46. "Mr. Muhammad, the archaeologist, directed much of his anger at President Bush. 'A country's identity, its value and civilization resides in its history,' he said. 'If a country's civilization is looted, as ours has been here, its history ends. Please tell this to President Bush. Please remind him that he promised to liberate the Iraqi people, but that this is not a liberation, this is a humiliation,'" John Burns, "Pillagers Strip Iraqi Museum of Its Treasure," *New York Times*, April 13, 2003.

47. Pitkin's survey of etymologies also says nothing of interests. She however concludes only that the etymology of freedom and liberty has many "complexities." Because of this complexity, she argues against those such as Berlin and Arendt who picked out only the features of etymology that suited their argument; Pitkin, "Are Freedom and Liberty Twins?" 546.

48. Hoad, *Etymology*, 182

49. And by extension of this suggestion, freedom would not have been granted reluctantly in the face of pressure from those who were not free but demanded it. That would return us again to the thesis of a freedom emerging because it was useful although this time it would be because such emancipation was in the interests of those elites facing serious resistance (e.g., Drake and McCubbins, "Origins," 12).

50. Liddell and Scott, *English–Greek Lexicon*, 215.

51. De Maistre, *Considerations*, 51.

52. Ibid.

2

Prerevolutionary Liberty

Long before the celebrated revolutions that marked the inauguration of *liberté*, the liberty of the people had been building steadily for centuries to the point where it had become a central theme of prerevolutionary politics. The problem with this prior liberty is that it looks nothing like that which was to come. Prerevolutionary liberty was chartered freedom, a right as grant, while the freedom of the revolutionaries was, they claimed, an inherent right or a right of man. This historical disjuncture is a problem because the political freedom that has been associated with the great, inaugural revolutions of the West requires that at least a fraction of the *same* type of freedom be prior. Only in that way can such freedom be secured, just as the revolutions happened to better secure the *a priori* or natural liberty of the English, American, and French peoples.

But in every case, prior to the Glorious, American, or French Revolutions, the freedom beforehand was nothing like that which was to come, which would imply, impossibly, that the free peoples and their freedom were impossible. The dilemma is deepened in this chapter with the full recovery and presentation of the dissimilar politics and theory of prerevolutionary liberty. Regretfully there is only enough space to render some interpretation of the liberty before that of the Glorious Revolution. To also describe political freedom before the American and the French revolutions would constitute a book all by itself. Where a note is possible, some mention of liberty by De Maistre, an often overlooked French thinker of prerevolutionary politics, or from the American Loyalists may be relayed in order to provide some hint of the liberty before the French and American revolutions as well. But what is presented henceforth is sufficient for the purpose of pointing out the instructive question that prerevolutionary freedom raises for the investigation of the origins of free peoples.

Some of the features of this older, prior liberty were that, perhaps until the very day of the revolution, it had attained such an advanced level that it was considered worthy of vociferous defense. Divine-right theory represented the apogee of a long era of prerevolutionary politics. But at the very height of its splendor a series of underhanded attacks (e.g., the Monmouth Rebellion) and radical criticisms (e.g., the Dissenters) threatened the fruits of that slow process. Filmer was, for example, extremely concerned about the emergence of "a liberty only to destroy liberty."[1] Astell was worried about the effect of self-seeking attacks from the Dissenters and urged their repression. The concerns of Filmer or Astell were not unreasonable because, in contrast to any novel and untested proposals for the so-called natural liberty of the people, prerevolutionary liberty had a tried and true method for its advancement that was accessible to every member of society. It was a potentially unlimited freedom in terms of its quantity and distribution, so much so that the legal and judicial institutions of the day were designed to brake this freedom lest it burst forth uncontrollably because of its very abundance. Indeed, even with these institutional checks to rationalize such liberty, and perhaps because of them, it was still widely distributed throughout society. Krieger notes, "[t]he institutions of chartered freedom, then, bequeathed a tradition of myriad rights, infinitely variable in degree and in kind, extending indiscriminately across the religious, social, economic, and political interests of men."[2]

The point of recalling prerevolutionary liberty in *The Origins of Free Peoples* is not immediately apparent. To be sure, any study of origins typically commences with some relevant survey of history or otherwise offers some acknowledgement of the past. But proponents such as Filmer or De Maistre, who are sometimes classified as fearsome political theorists of divine right, are not typically considered as the first references to consult for the history of free peoples. For example, in *Liberty before Liberalism*, Skinner unearths what he calls the "neo-Roman" theory of liberty.[3] Similar in spirit to the activist republican liberty of the city-states of the Italian Renaissance but stripped of its old objective of glory, proponents of neo-Roman liberty in seventeenth-century England emphasized the importance of citizen independence. But in order to actualize their liberty, neo-Roman citizens had to be free of domination, including potential domination. Following an interpretation of Roman law that distinguished between freedom and slavery, English proponents argued that the "mere possibility" of subjugation was slavery. To protect their liberty, citizens would need vigilant representatives as well as numerous guarantees and legal checks. Critics like Blackstone and Bentham soon undermined the neo-Roman idea as unworkable leaving the ideological field open for the liberal scheme that defended against physical not potential coercion.

Other commentators seeking the roots of free peoples typically turn to any source other than the divine right theorists. For instance, Nederman reaches back historically far beyond the seventeenth century to the twelfth century and discerns glimmers of freedom similar in intention and effect to what would be recognized today.[4] Nederman argues that John of Salisbury articulated a view of public liberty that was not necessarily uncommon for the day. Liberty of conscience, toleration, and dissent were to be expected of the virtuous citizen. What distinguished that conception from the freedom to come, especially the liberal view, was that the distinction between public and private spheres was unknown in the Middle Ages. Liberty of conscience was necessarily a form of "communal functionalism" that benefited society as a whole. John of Salisbury was admittedly "no John Stuart Mill" nevertheless "toleration of free thought and debate . . . did not have to wait until the dawn of the Renaissance, let alone the Enlightenment."

In contrast to Skinner's liberty before liberalism, which certainly adds to the knowledge base of seventeenth and eighteenth century English political controversies, or Nederman's startling medieval sourcing, the recollection of prerevolutionary liberty hones one's sensitivity to the origins of free peoples today. Indeed, unlike any other prior conception of freedom, from the medieval idea of immunities to the republican freedom of the Italian city-states, prerevolutionary liberty provokes an apprehensive, reflective search for what is necessary for free peoples to originate now. Whereas Skinner's neo-Roman liberty is explicitly recalled for readers as an enlightening alternative from another era, and as a lesson in the value of the historian's craft, the historical retrieval of prerevolutionary liberty triggers a helpful confrontation and a methodological reckoning. If such a history is rejected out of hand, then why it is so summarily rejected is a question that should be carefully answered by the reader. Such liberty should be considered defunct but why? Is it because its proponents evidently lost in the competitive marketplace of ideas? Was it because, as some have suggested, its patriarchalist foundations were philosophically incoherent? Or is prerevolutionary liberty to be rejected because of the evident historical point that its proponents decisively lost in revolutionary politics and war?

Generally, in addition to providing new data, the study of origins or genealogy contains a valuable combative component.[5] Nietzsche called his work a polemic, while Baudrillard often referred to the ideas of "challenge" and duel. They were in part provocateurs and didactically their methodology was not only to narrate their version of history but to provoke readers to lash out against their interpretations and to carefully reflect upon that reaction. Similarly, by the end of this chapter, the most valuable response to the provocation of prerevolutionary liberty as grant should be the declaration, "that is not how freedom arose!" With some indignation the reader should insist that the free peoples did not originate from such prerevolutionary roots. It should be avowed that proponents such as Filmer, Astell, De Maistre or the American Tories "do not deserve an entire chapter" in a book on the origins of free peoples. Even better would be an additional, nuanced response which insists that free peoples did not originate with that source but rather began from some other starting point. Such a response signals a first acknowledgment of the origins of free peoples as having a formula distinctive to them and imperative for their mode of freedom. Such a response signals the analytic recognition that such peoples and their type of freedom have their own rules of possibility that are not the rules of history, of war, of winning rhetoric, nor even of rationality. It is the indignant, perhaps insulted, but ultimately focused reaction upon necessity alone that opens the gate onto what Nietzsche once called the secret garden of origins.

Hypothesis

Surprisingly, the conception of prerevolutionary liberty begins with, of all political proponents, the thinkers of divine right. Sir Robert Filmer made sure to begin nearly all of his political works with some quotation emphasizing *libertas*. Joseph De Maistre mourned the "liberty" extinguished by the French Revolution. Mary Astell, although hailed today as an early feminist, sought freedom for her "ladies" not by challenging strong authority but by appealing to it.

 In the history of modern political thought, however, it has been presumed that the theory of the divine right of kings and its politics of royal absolutism threatened free peoples.[6] Figgis, along with others from the pluralist tradition such as Harold Laski and G. D. H. Cole, took special note of the implications of divine-right theory for the modern state and democratic freedoms centuries later.[7] Whitehead argued that the "freedom" that grew out of "original contract" and dismissed "the Stuarts into romance, founded the American Republic and brought the French Revolution" had "Divine Right of Kings" as its "antagonistic doctrine."[8] Along a similar vein, Berlin, who conducted a lengthy study of De Maistre, states that, "Maistre earns our gratitude as a prophet of the most violent, most destructive forces which have threatened and still threaten liberty and the ideals of normal human beings."[9] Most notably perhaps, Locke succinctly expressed the now-familiar polar opposition between free peoples and divine right when he argued that "a generation of men has sprung up among us, who would flatter Princes with an Opinion, that they have a Divine Right to absolute Power . . . To make way for this doctrine they have denied Mankind a Right to natural Freedom."[10]

But if the apparently fearsome theorists of divine right were once locked in a deadly ideological contest with revolutionaries and Dissenters espousing liberty and threatening regicide, it makes strategic sense that they might speak for liberty as well.[11] The divine-right theorists were nothing if not the most forceful, and desperate, apologists of prerevolutionary politics. If so, they had to speak well of its liberty. Hence if these prerevolutionary thinkers were wedded both to the most extreme expressions of royal absolutism and they also conceded the importance of liberty, then they must explain and even defend liberty in terms of their "supreme power." It is this older, nobler logic of free peoples that has yet to be systematically retrieved.

Perhaps the main reason for the alternating modern cycles of either neglect or outright denunciation of the divine-right thinkers is not because of their political theory of sovereignty so much as their defense of prerevolutionary liberty. A preliminary hypothesis can be offered here. First it is ideologically more effective, then as now, for proponents of a new, modern freedom to contrast it with the fearsome "absolute power" of the "divine right of kings" than to pedantically compare the advantages and disadvantages of one form of liberty against another. The latter, analytic, dry discussion would hardly make for exciting pamphleteering. As will be noted in the next chapter, the seventeenth century triumvirate of Algernon Sidney, James Tyrrell, and John Locke independently produced line by line critiques of Sir Robert Filmer's political writings. They were very much Filmer experts yet none mentioned his notion of liberty.

Second, the mode of revolutionary freedom propounded in the writings of Sidney, Tyrrell, Locke, and others has a sequential requirement that cannot be reconciled with the earlier type offered by divine-right theory. A prerevolutionary liberty that was too dissimilar from the freedom to come would not allow for the other, newer form to originate. No one could then speak about more firmly instituting rights of man, better securing self-evident truths, or more fully guaranteeing natural liberty.[12] Indeed, no one could then speak of the Glorious or French Revolutions (wrongly or rightly) as those celebrated events that secured the freedom to which the revolutionaries were already entitled, as though some such freedom had existed beforehand.[13] The revolutionary mode of freedom that motivated Milton, Locke, or Paine and inspired the great-grandchildren of such revolutions like Whitehead or Berlin has an inescapable sequential requirement. It must have a *similar* version of itself, however hazy, mythical, or intuitive, in its history. Otherwise no such freedom could ever become more firmly secured or better guaranteed by any revolution. The celebrated sort of people that have "natural liberty" as their starting point is not possible if a very different kind of liberty already sits chronologically in that slot. Unlike liberty as right, liberty as grant could not be advanced or secured by popular revolution but only by the continuing sufferance of the sovereign.

Sovereignty

The starting point for the recovery of prerevolutionary liberty begins with the concept of sovereignty. The divine-right theorists consistently distinguished sovereignty into two aspects, "right and exercise of right."[14] But only with the former term is the basis of their politics and their liberty identifiable. In divine-right thought, an orderly politics is said to originate with the most powerful human figure or with whoever has "right." To instead ask the more familiar modern questions of legitimacy, such as who has political right or who should have it, is to be focused mistakenly upon the proper "exercise of right." In an instructive example, De Maistre deploys the distinction in his polemic against the French revolutionaries. He states,

> [t]his is not the question. The question is not whether the French people can be *free* with the constitution they have but whether they can be *sovereign*. They change the question to escape the logic. Let us begin by excluding the exercise of sovereignty [*l'exercice de la souveraineté*] and insist on the fundamental point that the sovereign will always be in Paris, that all this noise about representation means nothing, that the *people* remain perfectly alien to government.[15]

De Maistre's concern was exclusively with the location of the sovereign and that reasoning led him to pose a question about the location of "the people." The question is a valid one, De Maistre could infer, as it was they who were so acclaimed by the revolutionaries as sovereign. Evidently, the response he received was less than adequate, for to speak only of the "representation" of the people is to answer a different kind of question about how their sovereignty, presumed, is to be best exercised. Like other divine-right theorists, so used to the splendid presence of a monarch, De Maistre could never see "the people." Try as he might, he could never locate that newly celebrated source of all political power.

The emphasis upon "right" or upon the location of the sovereign instead of the appropriate "exercise of right" is the converse of what is expected in more recent political reasoning. For instance, the pluralist and democratic thinker G. D. H. Cole insisted, as a fundamental principle, upon knowing "the *content* and purpose" of every political act.[16] Indeed, many political commentators today would be quite comfortable with a question such as whether adjusting a nation's constitution can bring a people freedom. It exemplifies a kind of familiar political science that seeks to "get the institutions right." This is the sort of modern reasoning that is understandable today, the kind that can suggest how we can secure the freedom that we like or that is thought to be useful.

Divine-right theory is practical as well because it emphasizes politics solely as a function of human endeavor. The difference is that such politics are not a function of what is proper to "man" or to humanity. Rather, politics is a function of what is determined as proper by the identifiable human who has all political right. As Pocock has noted, "that any law or right must have begun within human history is an argument for absolutism. If man made law he must have sovereign power; that power must descend to his heirs intact; all laws . . . must have been made by somebody."[17] For the divine-right thinkers, sovereignty is never abstract or conceptual but is, rather, always incarnate. Somebody is the sovereign; a human being has the right. That there must be an identifiable decision-maker makes for practical political theory and a historically sensitive one because it starts with the condition that politics, including the laws and liberty must have a demonstrably human source. The thinkers of divine right were necessarily strict political empiricists in that social order was a function of human practices not abstract dictates. This was because there was no location where decision-making was more recognizable, more "visible," terrible, or more "majestic" than at the site of a monarch. The very being of the king, exclaimed Filmer, is "power." It is much easier to identify the "original" of political order with the monarchical regime type than with any other.

The insistence on the embodiment of right is not diminished if the lineage or identity of the proper heir has been forgotten. To illustrate the point, Filmer sets up a thought experiment by noting that if Adam, that most obvious of sovereigns, were alive but ready to die now, "it is certain that there is one man, and but one in the world, who is next heir."[18] This corporeal fact is the case even if "the knowledge of who should be that one man be quite lost." In this example, it is not that the sovereign is missing but merely the knowledge of him that is lost. In terms of Filmer's absolutist mindset, there is never a question of confirming whether a monarch has political "right" legally or justly. That can only be a consideration if the focus is (erroneously) on the exercise of sovereignty. Whether the sovereign's title is certain or certified, whether the lineage can be traced back to Adam or not, is ultimately beside the point. Even a "usurper" can be sovereign in the basic sense of having "right," by his evidently identifiable and supremely powerful presence.

It is a polite gesture, perhaps, as a widespread expression of devotion, when a monarch is inaugurated in a ceremony that has been performed over centuries of tradition. But Filmer is adamant that such induction does not sanction or make legitimate.[19] "The election of kings is rather a formality than any real power." In this regard, Filmer noted Hooker's *Ecclesiastical Polity* (VIII, ii, 8) with some satisfaction. "Those public solemnities before mentioned [the coronations of Saul, David, or Solomon] do either serve for an open testification of the inheritor's right, or belongeth to the form of inducting him into possession of that thing he hath right unto."[20] A monarch's right to kingship, as the "right" of sovereignty, is already his. Inaugural affairs, however ancient or customary, do not imply a right to choose one's own rulers. "For we do not find the Israelites prayed that they themselves might choose their own king; they dreamed of no such liberty."[21] Typically, Filmer flies to the most extreme example to make his point and thereby clarifies his style of political reasoning. Filmer draws on the case of the child-king Joas, "a child but of seven years old," who was made the leader of ancient Israel. Now, by more familiar rules of what is optimal such a choice is absurd. "Woe to the land whose king is a child," agreed Filmer. Nevertheless Joas was made ruler and eventually his people were "rewarded" because he turned out to be the most religious king "that nation ever enjoyed." Filmer's stunning point: just because another act would have been more expedient is no reason for it. There is no *a priori* or natural right to choose one's sovereign and certainly none that derives from reasons of utility.

In short, Filmer's conception of sovereignty is the unwavering adherence to the view that where there are politics, a sovereign exists and must always be accounted for. "There is and always shall be continued to the end of the world, a natural right of a supreme father over every multitude, although by the secret will of God, many at first do most unjustly obtain the exercise of it."[22] Sovereignty never only exists conceptually or as a guiding idea, "for an heir there always is." The right of sovereignty, always localizable with somebody, is there and the person of the sovereign is also present.

When sovereignty as incarnate right is central, then politics revolves around publicizing or promoting the sovereign's location and presence as much as possible. Of course, it is just such promotion that led to critiques such as those in Tyrrell's *Patriarcha non Monarcha* or Voltaire's *Lettres philosophiques*, which found such politics to be part of a degrading and fearsome tendency toward "arbitrary power." But in divine-right thinking, while the accentuation of sovereignty might take many forms, it can never be through that notorious accumulation of power at the expense of others since no one else ever had it for it to be lost.[23] Indeed, Filmer expresses some puzzlement about that fearful view saying that "the new coined distinction of subjects into royalists and patriots is most unnatural, since the relation between king and people is so great that their well-being is reciprocal."[24] The arrogation of something called power to the monarch at the expense of Parliament, the Estates General, or "the people" requires that power be a scarce good in a zero-sum game. That certainly sounds like a familiar perspective now. Moderns instinctively understand the realist view that the accumulation of power is at the expense of competing interests. But this view can hardly be meaningful to prerevolutionary writers who are typically deemed as so different.

The sovereign of divine-right theory increases the extent of his presence through coronation, self-promotion, and in myriad other ways. An example of this accentuation process is to be found in the genre of autobiographical self-promotion in order to cultivate an enduring presence. The posthumous publication of Charles Stuart's *Eikon Basilike*, a tender, "spiritual autobiography," allegedly written during his imprisonment, generated such widespread sympathy that the book was credited with the "restoration of the royal family" in England.[25] The *Basilikon Doron* of King James I, as his "majesties instructions to his dearest sonne," provides a different example of a royal modality devoted to the accentuation of sovereign right.[26] It too was dedicated to enhancing the stable presence of the sovereign for the effect of following those instructions is to further center the sovereign's location by encouraging the appearance of assurance or of seeming at ease in any circumstance. The reader quickly notices that there is never too much immersion in any one discipline. From the games that the young Henry should play, to the foods that he should eat, to the speed of his gesticulations, the total effect of James's instructions to the future sovereign is an unbroken line of "moderation" and a disposition of unruffled presence in any situation, however transitory. Hence, even when circumstances appear troubling, the being of the sovereign is nevertheless immutable and observable.[27]

In these ways, which extend his magnificence and visibility, a sovereign can be said to be gathering power unto himself. Such personalism is just what modern critics would expect. After all, the threats of absolute power and willfulness were in part why Locke, Paine, Cole, Laski, Whitehead, and Berlin worried that "divine right" was incompatible with freedom. But it is also how the converse can be imagined; namely, that freedom can only be possible through just such sovereignty, for in a politics of divine right there would simply be no other way to achieve it. Indeed, in order to imagine this other effect of sovereignty, it helps to remain with the worst modern expectations of a Filmer or a De Maistre in this regard. Precisely because their visions have become so unacceptable, one has only to burden these thinkers once more with their boldest notion of sovereignty. On such a reading, nothing political could happen without the supreme power. The principle is so pivotal that it would even have to be applied to conceptions of democracy.[28] Of course, their principle of "right" would also have to be central to prerevolutionary liberty. And in turn, the practice of such liberty would have to accentuate sovereign right.

Liberty as Grant

There are numerous, approving, references to "liberty" in the second half of Filmer's *Patriarcha*; in many of Filmer's other works, especially his *Free-Holder's Grand Inquest*; in various sections of De Maistre's *Considerations*; and in Astell's feminist and antidissent writings.[29] Of course, such an emphasis could only be the case if to speak of such liberty was still to speak of sovereignty. Sovereignty was essentially all that these thinkers could discuss. Yet the writings of these absolutists, in response to the character of dissent that they confronted, were also heavily infused with ideas of liberty. Their view of political liberty is disconcerting in that it goes quite against any notion of freedom as secured by law or as guaranteed natural rights. Furthermore, their older, nobler liberty was not universally applicable. It was always crafted specifically for personal or group requests and so was different in every case.[30] Indeed, prerevolutionary liberty was always so specific that it meant getting exactly what you requested. Such freedom was never simply already prior. One could not just pick it up because it was somehow, perhaps intuitively or naturally, already one's birthright and develop it further. Instead there were always political procedures for such liberty that depended upon the monarch and the implications of his or her supreme power. The people's rights, De Maistre once noted, were all concessions of a sovereign that were historically verifiable.[31]

The seemingly paradoxical relation between freedom and royal absolutism is best illustrated in Filmerian terms, thanks to the forcefulness of his expression. His infamous notion of "arbitrary power," as the sovereign's unfettered right to act and to take back that act, was not so much a threat to freedom as the key to it.[32] Specifically, when the notion was related to law, and especially to countermanding unjust law, arbitrary power was crucial to liberty. In Filmer's absolutist theory, the sovereign continuously sustains all law.[33] But the sovereign can also withdraw his sanction, his supreme power, from this or that law at any time, seemingly arbitrarily. All that is happening, of course, is that the sovereign is holding back his own exercise of the absolute power in a specific area for someone in particular. How like a father to restrain himself for the sake of his children. He leaves them a bit of the nourishing power so that they can live and even flourish. Freedom is essentially such a "provision" and stems from an interruption of the force of "law." Indeed, without the attentive, fatherly intercessions of Filmer's sovereign, without such "relief," the force of law becomes unreasonable and "tyrannical."

As an exemption from law, the liberty of divine-right theory was simultaneously a "provision" or specific grant of absolute power. Obeying a kind of physics of conservation of power, there could never be a diminution of "absoluteness" or of such "complete" or "whole" power.[34] As such, it could even be said to animate all existence.[35] When freeing others, the sovereign of divine-right theory merely interrupted his own exercise of it. It remained absolute power for all that. Always working at full strength, it has to at all times be located with somebody. And if the monarch is refraining from wielding (some of) it, then somebody else must be doing so. That again is what the incarnate principle of "right" demanded. It must always be located somewhere with a human sovereign. De Maistre highlighted what he called "*liberty through the monarchy*" and noted that through it many subjects receive a "portion" of sovereignty.

There are two degrees of liberty that can stem from such redirection of the supreme power. The first is what Jean Bodin, a much earlier proponent of sovereignty, called "natural libertie" and is broadly illustrative of the liberty as provision type.[36] It was the basic or empirical form of such liberty and was evidenced by the fact that everyone had been granted it because they continued to live. A philosophy of absolutism can suggest no other way to explain their ongoing existence.[37] What could be called Filmer's natural patriarchalism provides an example in this regard.[38] When

Filmer referred to Adam in *Genesis* as the world's first and most obvious sovereign, it was because Adam was then the only human in existence, or more precisely, because he was not prevented from existing. Lovingly, God was refraining from wielding all of his absolute power for Adam's sake.[39] The very existence of Adam was how Filmer knew that he was bequeathed with sovereignty in this world. Hence any living man or woman who arrived after Adam must be a function of Adam's own fatherly self-restraint. For a Filmer, the very existence, much less the prosperity of any man, came from the sovereign who must be refraining from the full exercise of his absolute power.

But Bodin's "natural libertie" is not only the type that permits subjects their lives, as though that were not enough. It is also the type that allows them their property or "goods." Bodin seems to have called such liberty "natural" because without it the basic function and continuation of human life would be impossible. The application of such natural "libertie" can be seen in Bodin's distinction between a royal and lordly monarch when he notes that the "[r]oyal monarch or king is he which placed in sovereignty yielded himself as obedient unto the laws of nature as he desireth his subjects to be towards himself, leaving unto every man his natural liberty, and the propriety of his own goods."[40] As with all thinkers of sovereignty, Bodin related all political topics to the supreme power. In this case, the royal monarch "yielded himself as obedient" to the "laws of nature." He is not politically subject to such laws but thoughtfully limits his intervention into what is necessary for the continuation of the basic functions. Even these natural laws then (laws of the natural because life would be impossible without them) remain contingent upon sovereign discretion.

For Bodin, how a sovereign decides to address natural liberty merely determines the classification of his monarchy. That only this typological implication is emphasized serves as an indicator of the passing regard Bodin had for such liberty. For instance, Bodin notes another sort of monarch, one who is not as benevolent as the "royal" type. Such reign will have to be suffered. To continue with the aforementioned passage:

> the difference of a Lordly Monarch, who may be a just and virtuous prince, and equally govern his subjects, being himself yet nevertheless lord both of their persons and goods. And if it so chance the Lordly Monarch having justly conquered his enemy's country, to set them again at liberty, with the propriety of their goods; of a lord he becommeth a king, and changeth the Lordly Monarchy into a Monarchy Royal.[41]

In this example of a king and a conquered people, the monarch exercises a harsher style of rule because the lordly monarch is not as lenient as the royal type. "And if it so chance" that the monarch again permits the unfortunates their natural liberty, then he becomes the "royal" type of king. But either way the right was his in terms of the logic of sovereignty.[42] The lordly monarch, notes Bodin, is just, virtuous, and "equally" governor in every way. Indeed, the lordly monarch is the more "durable" type and appears more "majestical" by contrast with his subjects because they "hold not their lives, goods, and libertie."

However this natural liberty, obviously so very necessary, was nevertheless not enough for the prerevolutionary political theorists. Bodin was not engaged in a deadly contest over liberty and so he barely developed the idea in his *République*. Happily, his main concern was to elucidate his novel concept of sovereignty and how it influenced and stabilized various regime types. But the divine-right theorists all faced insistent contenders who thought, wrote, and spoke of "liberty" with its distasteful implications of resistance and even regicide. In a bidding war with the Dissenters of England or with the French Revolutionaries, these absolutist defenders had to offer up more than just such basic liberty. To have only spoken, then, of freedom in the form of Bodin's natural liberty would have been a poor ideological proposal indeed. The additional freedom that the prerevolutionary theorists defended was also a provision. But there was more than mere life to be had by it.

Tyranny of the Laws

The exact procedure for prerevolutionary liberty begins with a theme found throughout the history of political thought: that of the lawgiver. But where Aristotle, Rousseau, or Montesquieu, with that typical philosophers' prejudice, praise the foresight of the lawgiver, the divine-right theorist only requires his "supreme power." "True legislators," De Maistre stated, "are never what are called scholars."[43] The divine-right theorists denied that law emerges from political knowledge. For De Maistre, the "talent" for "knowledge" that is peculiar to philosophers such as "Montesquieu" or "Bacon" is the "proof" that they do not have the other talent to give law. De Maistre considered "reasoning" to be too weak to grasp the complex requirements of a society. So its use in constructing a fitting constitution could only be a farce. It could only be a "schoolboy composition." A touted exemplar of lawgiving such as Lycurgus simply set down law. Similarly, Filmer insisted that law was fathered rather than deduced from what was intellectually determined as fitting.[44] The making of law, like the first creation, requires the "supreme power." This is why even Solon's highly regarded regime of laws was so short lived. According to Filmer, Solon had obviously lacked such supreme power because he came only from the "middle class."

The source of the laws in the supreme power or the sovereign means that what is lawful must always originate anew. There is no contiguous, "ancient," or even mythological history of a national constitution such that the legal historian could automatically observe a similar act in the past that drives or serves as a precedent for the event in question. Rather, since the politics of divine right are always a matter of the absolute power of the sovereign, the history of law is one of dissimilarity and interruption. As Filmer noted, "for every custom there was a time when it was no custom . . . When every custom began, there was something else than custom that made it lawful." Conservative thinkers like Filmer, De Maistre, (and even the mercurial Burke) have often been cast as stubbornly beholden to habit or custom.[45] But for the divine-right theorists, as the most consistent of absolutists, what is "lawful" derives not from the accumulated weight of thoughtless habit but from "something else" that is the "superior power."

But if the concept of sovereignty helps to address the origins of law in prerevolutionary thought, what of the origins of liberty? The critics of "divine right" are often concerned with precisely such supreme power and its extension in the unchecked use of force. The divine-right thinkers could not simply table this concern as a question of the exercise of right and so, outside of their purview. In the menacing context of dissent, Filmer was only too aware of "those men who say that it is a dangerous and slavish condition to be subject to the will of any one man who is not subject to the laws." The absolutist rejoinder is as disconcerting as it is disarming. The divine-right theorists challenged the security of the laws. Filmer chided those worried about the safety of the people's liberties. "Such men consider not," he warned, the "tyranny of the laws." Addressing or redressing the danger of unjust law was the prerevolutionary path to the people's liberties.

The focus on the sovereign seems to have made the divine-right thinkers skeptical about almost everything else. That included, incredibly enough, the safety and pre-eminence of the laws (hailed today as the "rule of law"). Rather, law was installed merely because the monarch could not be everywhere at once, as for example, when he was overseas conducting a battle campaign.[46] Hence, because "every private person could not have access to their persons to learn their will and pleasure, then of necessity laws were invented." Filmer recognizes that the king is normally "*lex locunus*—speaking law." Nevertheless "published" law can supplement "obscure" laws and mitigate those laws that were overly "rigourous." By these means, through the written laws, "both king and people were in many things eased."

Filmer's view of law, then, takes published law as a mere means and as something to be guided rather than as a guide. Nodding with savage respect, Filmer admits that such guidance "requires profound abilities of nature" on the part of the monarch.[47] But at least the laws remain subject to human judgment and therefore to some appeal. Without the sovereign's attentive exceptions, the law by itself is "no better than a tyrant, since *summum jus* [law pushed to extremes] is *summa injuria* [extreme injustice]." The king must constantly remain "above" the laws "for the good only of them that are under the laws, and to defend the people's liberties."[48] Whenever the divine-right thinkers conceded that their monarch obeyed the laws, this meant obedience only to the "*upright laws*, and that with discretion and mercy."[49] Filmer is quick to point out that the king need not observe any "evil and unjust laws." Indeed, at his coronation, the king "swears to abolish" the latter. "The safety of the people," says Filmer, "is an exception implied in every monarchical promise."[50] Like a gardener pruning weeds, the job of the king is to veto evil laws and thus to continually dispense "justice." Not much earlier, King James I had taken special care to emphasize and protect precisely this aspect of his rule.

Thus, as a type of exemption, the liberty of divine-right theory relies upon the interruption of law.[51] Specifically, prerevolutionary liberty begins with a judgment against unjust law. But how does a law, evidently just at some point since the sovereign allowed it, become unjust? Such an outcome is constructed politically and Filmer cannot help but acknowledge this fact. Filmer is aware of the familiar truism that the laws cannot be explicit in every case.[52] But such a problem cannot be attributed to a legal code that is deficient in itself, say, because it did not account for some foreseeable eventuality.[53] Nor can a deficiency in law emerge because it does not correspond to some philosophical or mythical standard of foresight. A problem of law only originates through a particular political interplay that, as usual, centers upon the sovereign. Filmer was fond of the Aristotelian reasoning that, "where there is a gap it should be corrected or supplied, as if the lawmaker himself were present to ordain it."[54] But for Filmer, such a gap is not in the law. Rather, like anything else in the politics of divine right, such a gap appears only through the efforts of the supreme power. All politics, law, liberty, perhaps even all being, must at all times be fathered.

Examples

The first element needed for prerevolutionary liberty was the grievance. It began the process of the development of a problem in the laws that might then require redress and liberty. A grievance typically arose from the enforcement of a specific law that was supported by that terrible, absolute power and became intolerable to those subjected to it. Given the prerevolutionary mindset, this could not mean for every "individual" or "person" in society. It meant intolerable for those subjects who complained that they had come to feel the weight of some law or laws. It was then up to the sovereign to rectify such injury. But for there to be any chance of such liberty, the grievance had to first come to his or her attention. Hence, the important formal requirement of prerevolutionary liberty was the petition. For example, Astell's prescriptive writings deploy precisely this procedure for freedom.[55] They bring a complaint to the queen about the tyrannical force of custom and law on a specified group. And they suggest redress through a call for the sovereign's intervention. In Astell's particular example, she proposed a place for women to retire from societal pressures that were exacerbated by unjust laws. Astell's petition is a textbook example of a prerevolutionary effort to effect liberty. Furthermore, as an absolutist writer, Astell accentuated the potential for such freedom by defending its source in the supreme power of her queen. Thus, in taking both her feminist and conservative positions, Astell was not in any way contradictory.

For instance, Astell's *Serious Proposal to the Ladies* fits well with her *Reflections on Marriage* in terms of the grievance–redress mode of prerevolutionary liberty. In the latter text, Astell identifies the lack of education for women as one of the main causes of unhappy marriages. This often results in the poor choice of a husband or, to use Astell's phrase, of a "Monarch for life."[56] Astell argues that, prior to marriage, men and women are equally subjects.[57] But women are customarily not educated, and so they are susceptible to react quickly to men's "flatteries" and be diverted by frivolous, short-term concerns. Education provides the moderation and reserve that allows for a more cautious assessment of a possible mate. So in her *Serious Proposal*, Astell suggests to "the Ladies" that they give some thought to becoming educated.[58] Her prescription is "to erect a *Monastery*" or a place for meditative "retirement" where women could learn how to act as an obedient subject of God.[59] Presumably, after such retirement in quiet friendship and contemplation, Astell's ladies will emerge as better wives, mothers, and judges of character.

"What now remains, but to reduce to Practice that which tends so very much to our advantage." In Part 2, therefore, as the practical section of the *Serious Proposal*, Astell bypasses Parliament and pleads her case directly to her sovereign. Thus:

> To her Royal Highness THE Princess ANN of Denmark... What was at first adress'd to the Ladies in General . . . not being ill receiv'd by them . . . now presumes on a more particular Application to Her who is the Principal of them, and whose Countenance and Example may reduce to Practice, what it can only Advise and Wish.

All of the elements of a petition for liberty can be found here. They include a grievance by a particular group (the proposal thus far not "ill receiv'd by them," i.e., by "the Ladies") addressed to the "Principal" and sovereign. Astell's "Advice" brings the proposal to the attention of Her Majesty and it is carefully framed as a "Wish." Furthermore, Astell knows that this is the right personage to petition since, "I consider you Madam as a Princess who is sensible that the Chief Prerogative of the great is the Power they have of doing . . . Good."

There are at least two reasons why Astell can know to address her petition to the princess. First, Astell recognizes that the source of liberty is the sovereign. Generally, Astell is reluctant to use the word liberty, perhaps because of its deployment by her political opponents.[60] But when she does speak positively of liberty, it is always in the same breath with monarchy.[61] She notes, for example, that "the Liberties not of this or that Nation or Region only" would all disappear without the queen or without "such a universal Benefactress." Astell also states that the "Liberties of our own English nation" came through "our monarch." Indeed Astell went so far as to claim that the "Great Queen . . . gives Laws and Liberties to *Europe*."[62]

The other reason that Astell can turn to Princess Ann for liberty stems from her research, in contrast to the biases of the day, showing that women can be sovereign too. Astell spends some time developing this point and finds numerous examples from the Old Testament and elsewhere where such matriarchy has been the case. These instances, Miriam and the Queen of Sheba among them, undercut the "pretence of *natural inferiority*" of women that prevailed in the misogynist literature of the day.[63] Thus, when women do "have the supreme Authority, it is no Usurpation, nor do they act contrary to Holy Scripture, nor consequently to the Law of Nature." For Astell therefore, a woman can be sovereign and sovereignty is the source of politics and freedom. Astell was thus most correct in her effort to petition for liberty.

Filmer had similar ideas about how to proceed for liberty but with a different, less feminine, constituency in mind. For both petitioner and petitioned, the best way to get a hearing and to draw forth a problem of the laws was through a petition in Parliament. "Great are the advantages which both the king and people may receive by a well ordered parliament." Of course, the prerevolutionary theorists could not see such a body as anything other than consultative.[64] After all, any "liberties" it claims are by the ongoing grace of a monarch.[65] Furthermore it is his call, in England as in France, that brings the parliamentarians together.[66] Fortunately, a consultative forum was all that was needed for prerevolutionary liberty. Filmer argued that freedom results from such consultation since petitions could then be heard by the monarch and, in response, any royal grants of sovereignty could be "approbated" by the petitioners there.

Filmer argued that Parliament, in tandem with the king, maintains a rational distribution of freedom. Parliament, noted Filmer, is the forum that makes possible "what otherwise they [his Majesty, set in the plural] would not yield to."[67] It seems that exemptions would "otherwise" not be yielded because, without Parliament, there would be less chance that petitions, indicators of the people's "vexations," could come to the attention of the monarch. In the prerevolutionary political world, a lack of liberty was never due to any stinginess on the part of sovereign. Rather, the tendency of liberty must necessarily lean toward abundance. The sovereign of divine-right theory has so much power that he literally drops some of it or leaves some liberty lying about. Sounding strangely like Bentham, De Maistre suggested that monarchy is the regime type that can give the "most distinctions" to the "greatest number."[68] For instance, a monarch might give exemptions wholesale, as upon his coronation when granting a great number of them was traditional. "The pardons upon his accession are but the bounty of the prerogative."[69] Indeed the odd constitutional problem that these extreme absolutists faced was how to dampen the bias toward liberty.

For Filmer, Parliament both puts a brake on grants of freedom and maintains their possibility. First, as a major forum for airing grievances (another was the Star Chamber), it puts a physical limit on the number of petitions heard. Parliament sets this limit simply because it convenes at a specific time and place and so not every request can be heard. Second, the few "liberties" that Parliament had been granted for it to function generate healthy institutional jealousy. It allowed for a tension with the monarch in a way that conserved his power and therefore the potential for liberty as provision. In his *Patriarcha*, Filmer presents an illustrative interpretation of such tension in which the "Commons" and the king both worked to preserve the possibility of liberty (i.e., the monarch's capacity to make legal exemptions).[70] Parliament asked that the "council of the king should not, after the end of its session, make any ordinance against the common law." The king coyly responded that his power might be used at any time but with circumspection just as it had always been "before this time, so as the regality of the king be saved." On Filmer's reading, Parliament's request was not a jealous complaint about its prerogatives, as if it had any of its own.[71] Rather, its request had the considerate effect of reminding the king to hold on to more of his "regality" thereby preserving the rich future potential for English liberties. Apparently, any tension between king and Parliament helped to ration liberty in Filmer's England. This, along with the limitation that the physical space and time of Parliament placed on the number of petitions that could be received allowed for a general legal stability. The laws were thus "ordinarily maintained lest subjects be convented before the king and his council without just cause."[72] Hence, "Parliaments express his majesty, address him with petitions and by their consent and approbation do strengthen all the laws that the king, at their request . . . shall ordain."[73]

For the lucky petitioners, "once a petition is granted, it is in turn approbated by the petitioners who take on the necessary power and exercise it themselves." When the petitioners consent to the monarch's particular grant of sovereignty, they have thereby helped to create what Filmer termed a "paction."[74] It is the English version of De Maistre's tempting proposal that through liberty one receives a portion of the sovereign's power. The petitioners, in exercising their new liberty, become intimately involved in the execution of particular laws. Of course, they already had a hand in suggesting the new legislation through their petition. Once granted, they then "consent" to what they had requested. The exercise of their liberty then comes in acting exactly as they wished, as according to their petition, and in so doing they are obeying the newly ordained laws. In their hold of that portion of sovereignty and by acting according to the corrected laws, they themselves "do strengthen" the laws. The laws, then, are not only improved, but the petitioners also act freely in obeying them.

Ramifications

It turns out that liberty is as crucial to understanding the position of the divine-right theorists in the history of Western political thought as has been their fearsome notion of sovereignty. With only a bit of political insight, and with the cool of hindsight, what at first glance seems like a paradoxical relation between divine-right theory and liberty easily comes to seem ideologically reasonable, if not necessary. Sir Robert Filmer intuitively sensed that addressing the matter of "liberty" was important, it being a "question never yet disputed, though most necessary in these Times."[75] Perched at the precipice of revolution, the divine-right theorists recognized both the centrality and the attraction of the theme of liberty in the discourse of their opponents and they naturally sought to counter its siren song with their own defense. Their suggestion was essentially liberty as grant, while the liberty of the revolutionaries and Dissenters was, they professed, a natural right or a "right of man."

On the other side, for the freedom of the revolutionaries, or the "people's freedom," the past presented a delicate challenge. Revolutionary claims to inherent rights, to states of nature, or to natural rights were not simply legal claims or even myths about their respective national histories but were rather an inescapable prerequisite of the mode of liberation that they championed. For the revolutionaries, their history must contain an inkling of the freedom to come otherwise securing it more firmly made no sense. This is a structural necessity of the new freedom and the point is invariably born out in the documents of some of the most famous revolutionaries themselves, whether in Locke's *Two Treatises*, in the *Declaration of the Rights of Man*, or even in Jefferson's *Declaration of Independence*, all of which relied on claims to a prior freedom that could later be institutionally secured. Indeed, so pivotal is the requirement of affinity between what came before and what came after the great revolutions that even pseudoarguments such as "self-evident" truths, states of nature, and sheer presumption were sufficient so long as the earlier versions of freedom were similar. The sequential priority was for there to be at least some such freedom previously lying about for only then could it ever more fully blossom. Did not the French Revolutionaries, in their cries for *liberté*, instead mean more of the freedom that they already possessed? After all, it was because those rights had been trampled upon that they had to dismantle the *ancien régime* and institute their liberty more securely. The celebrated notion of the "rights of man" meant they had always been free beforehand. The abuses of the *ancien régime* only forced them to make that freedom, presumably implicit, explicit. Much the same could also be said for that liberty associated with what many still call, following a Whiggish reading, the Glorious Revolution.[76] In Locke's *Two Treatises*, to take what has been the best known theoretical expression of that event, liberty did not begin *ex nihilo*.[77] Rather, some of it was already lying about in what he called the "state of nature." Hence, when Locke's Englishmen installed William as constitutional monarch and eventually solidified representative government as a result, they could be seen as fully instituting what freedom they already had.[78]

As the most systematic critic of the new liberty, and as perhaps the clearest defender of the old one, Sir Robert Filmer pounced upon his opponents' most pivotal or imperative sequential prerequisite. Filmer knew that the Dissenters who threatened the order of his day needed at least some similar liberty to be prior. So he, like De Maistre and Astell, mercilessly criticized the novel and unverifiable thesis of the people's prior, natural liberty.[79] In particular, Filmer systematically attacked all notions of a primal, free state of nature that he found in the contractarian theories of Grotius, Bellarmine, Suarez, and Hobbes. Filmer understood that without some of the same freedom beforehand, however hazy or mythical, the individuals of Hobbes's or Grotius's schemes could not be said to contract together and more fully institutionalize their (prior) freedom.[80] Filmer's opponents would then also find their exhortations to resist the sovereign and their claims to have a pre-existing right to do so undermined.

The other response of the divine-right theorists was, of course, their defense of prerevolutionary liberty. Such liberty was perhaps the most dangerous argument that could be set against the opposition for their defense not only offered an ideological alternative of lovely liberty but was chronologically positioned such that it would precisely block the emergence of the revolutionary mode of freedom. The problem for a politics that relies upon some bit of same liberty to be prior to the revolution that secures it is that the historical record then suggests just the opposite. Thus the divine-right thinkers also admitted that there had long been freedom for the people. But the freedom before the Glorious Revolution was not so much like that of the state of nature (with individuals as natural rights bearers) but was rather a dissimilar type that arose from a royal gift. Where Locke saw staunch opposition to liberty, namely, in Filmer's notorious politics of "divine right," was a gentle and generous form of liberty. And in the freedom before the French Revolution, there was no legal evidence of the "rights of man," but there was a time tested mode of liberty applied by its princes.

The same historical discrepancy is even to be found in the American context, a context that Arendt exaggerated as exceptional and different from other great modern revolutions of the West.[81] The prerevolutionary logic of liberty was why, for example, American Loyalists such as Galloway or Boucher worried about the loss of American liberties should the British sovereign be denied by the independence faction who had dubbed themselves patriots. Galloway decried it as, "[t]he black scheme of independence."[82] On the Loyalist reading, to definitively challenge the British sovereign was a short-sighted form of blasphemy against the very power that sustained American liberty. After all, not only their liberties but the very existence of the American colonies legally depended upon royal grants of charters. The importance of such charters is illustrated by the now whimsical Charter Oak Affair in which Connecticut's leaders hid their charter inside an oak tree until the royal representative who had arrived to retrieve the charter and dissolve the colony grew frustrated in the search and returned home.[83]

It is no wonder, then, that prerevolutionary liberty has been ignored since the revolutionary mode of freedom and those peoples who subscribe to it would have been impossible otherwise. Interestingly, the same efforts to expunge such prior liberty continue.[84] There is certainly no mention of it in today's middle school history textbooks. Of course, *ancien régime* specialists and political historians of Europe's early modern era are aware of prerevolutionary liberty but, oddly in this era of copious scholarship on the question of freedom, no full length study of the form exists. It is because prerevolutionary liberty sets up a chronology that remains unacceptable, even today. It impeded what was sequentially necessary for the emergence of the celebrated freedom of some three great modern revolutions.[85] It is an eminently political question as to whether the history of political thought continues to be kept amenable in this all too important case.

Notes

1. Filmer, *Patriarcha and Other Writings*, 4.
2. Krieger, "Stages," 7.
3. Skinner, *Liberty*, 96, 72.
4. Nederman, "Principles," 67. Others find the roots of liberty even farther back in time. In their *Brief History of Liberty*, a text that eschews study of "theorizing" about liberty in favor of liberty itself, Schmidtz and Brennan argue at some length that freedom was available during the prehistoric era of the Neanderthals.

5. Consigny, "Nietzsche's Reading," 6–8.

6. For example, Burgess insists that divine-right theory "was not a language appropriate for addressing specific legal questions involving prerogatives and liberties," Burgess, *Absolute Monarchy*, 121.

7. Figgis, *The Divine Right of Kings*, 263; Laski, *Studies in the Problem of Sovereignty*, 222; Cole, "The Principle of Function," 60–67.

8. Whitehead, "Aspects of Freedom," 55–56.

9. Berlin, Introduction, xxxiii.

10. Locke, *Two Treatises*, 142.

11. See Harris, "Lives, Liberties and Estates," 227.

12. "Those responsible for the Revolution of 1688–89 justified their actions by invoking posterity, claiming that the liberties and religion of unborn generations were now safeguarded for all time," Jones, "Revolution in Context," 48.

13. "To this day, many historians hail the Glorious Revolution as a major victory in the battle against feudal hierarchy, the consequence—and guarantor—of British liberty," Perry, "Mary Astell," 445. "When James II left England, the English declared that this flight was an abdication: it is since then that they have been free," Constant, *Political Writings*, 304.

14. Filmer, *Patriarcha and Other Writings*, 21.

15. De Maistre, *Considerations*, 37. In *The Anarchy of a Limited or a Mixed Monarchy*, Filmer addresses the exact same issue with the same words: "that is not the question," Filmer, *Patriarcha and Other Writings*, 132.

16. "The policy of every political association must be guided by 'the *content* and purpose of the act.'" This principle, "flows as a necessary consequence from the denial of state sovereignty and omnicompetence," Cole, "The Social Theory," 96.

17. Pocock, *Ancient Constitution*, 189–90.

18. Filmer, *Patriarcha and Other Writings*, 10.

19. Ibid., 171.

20. Ibid., 19.

21. Ibid., 24.

22. Ibid., 11.

23. Astell, *Political Writings*, 174.

24. Filmer, *Patriarcha and Other Writings*, 5.

25. De Maistre, *Considerations*, 110.

26. James I, *The Political Works*, 46.

27. De Maistre, *Considerations*, 31.

28. Sommerville, *Politics and Ideology*, 34.

29. "The characteristics of the springtime of liberty are so striking that it is impossible to be mistaken. It is a time when love of the fatherland is a religion and respect for the laws a superstition . . . when everything, even crime, carries the mark of greatness," De Maistre, *Considerations*, 38.

30. Harding, "Political Liberty in the Middle Ages," 424.

31. De Maistre, *Considerations*, 50.

32. Astell, *Political Writings*, 136.

33. See Burgess, *Absolute Monarchy*, 95.

34. Daly, "The Idea of Absolute Monarchy," 231.

35. De Maistre, *Considerations*, 2; Garrard, "Joseph De Maistre's Civilization," 444.

36. Bodin, *Commonweale*, 204.

37. The "notion of a compact omnicompetent sovereign, by whose permission alone existed the right to breathe, was mixed up with the divine right of kings," Figgis, *Divine Right*, 122.

38. Filmer, *Patriarcha and Other Writings*, 60. Other types of patriarchalism include "anthropological" and "ideological," Schochet, *The Authoritarian Family*, 11–15.

39. An extensive survey of this usage of "absolute power" is traced in Oakley, "The Absolute and Ordained Power," 674.

40. Bodin, *Commonweale*, 204.

41. Ibid., 204.

42. Cragg, *Freedom*, 63.

43. De Maistre, *Considerations*, 52.

44. Filmer, *Patriarcha and Other Writings*, 44.

45. Brenkert, *Political Freedom*, 33, 63; Figgis, *Divine Right*, 254.

46. Filmer, *Patriarcha and Other Writings*, 41.

47. Ibid., 46.

48. Ibid., 44.

49. Ibid., 43.

50. Ibid., 149.

51. By contrast, "[t]he order that the judge is expected to maintain is . . . the regularity of a process resting on an expectation of non-interference . . . he must rule in a flow of the same order of actions . . . a going order," Hayek, *Law, Legislation, and Liberty*, vol. 2, *The Mirage of Social Justice*, 116.

52. Ibid., 46.

53. For instance, "laws . . . in their own nature are dumb and always need a judge to pronounce sentence," ibid., 153.

54. Ibid.

55. Astell, *Political Writings*, 31.

56. Ibid., 48.

57. Ibid., 26.

58. Astell, *A Serious Proposal*, 3, 6.

59. Ibid, 14.

60. Perry, "Mary Astell," 447.

61. For example, "GOD was pleas'd to restore our Monarch . . . and the Liberties of the *English* nation," Astell, *Political Writings*, 141.

62. Ibid., 30.

63. Ibid., 25; Schochet, *Authoritarian Family*, 218; Lister, "Marriage and Misogyny," 44.

64. Astell, *Political Writings*, 171.

65. Filmer, *Patriarcha and Other Writings*, 55; Rocquain, *The Revolutionary Spirit*, 106.

66. Sommerville, *Royalists and Patriots*, 171; Gottschalk, "French Parlements," 109.

67. Filmer, *Patriarcha and Other Writings*, 53. .

68. De Maistre, *Considerations*, 89.

69. Filmer, *Patriarcha and Other Writings*, 44.

70. Ibid., 50.

71. Ibid., 162.

72. Ibid., 51.

73. Ibid., 30.

74. Ibid., 55.

75. Ibid., 131.

76. Cruickshanks, *Glorious Revolution*, 1.

77. Schwoerer, "Locke, Lockean Ideas," 532.

78. Thus, "it was insisted that in terminating the kingship of James II and transferring the crown to William and Mary, the nation had acted by the authority and according to the forms of the ancient constitution: of King, Lords and Commons, the common law and its judges, extending back through Magna Carta to the Norman Conquest and beyond," Pocock, "Introduction," xii. Locke's "aim is of course to legitimate Whig revolution and reconstitution of a civil liberty commonwealth," Tully, *An Approach*, 304.

79. De Maistre, "De l'état de nature," 7: 563.

80. "'Tis often asked as a mighty Objection, *Where are*, or ever were, *any Men in such a state of Nature?*" Locke, *Two Treatises*, §14.

81. Arendt, *On Revolution*, 218.

82. Galloway, *A Reply*, 5.

83. Dye, et al., *Politics in America*, 56.

84. Tully, *An Approach*, 286–7.

85. Sommerville, *Politics and Ideology*, 38; Burgess, *Absolute Monarchy*, 97.

3

That Other Liberty

So what of the origins of that *other* freedom; that is, what are the origins of that modality typically associated with the great revolutions of the West and the peoples that celebrate them? Few subscribers to freedom as their paramount value would today countenance the claim that their freedom begins not as an inherent right but rather as a royal grant or charter. Therefore some other origins must be at work for those other free peoples. In the last chapter it was recalled that the liberties of the English, French, and even the American peoples were grants by their sovereign according to the various petitions made to them. If that answer to the question of origins seems unacceptable or unrecognizable, then that is only part of the problem to now be resolved. The other, harder problem raised by prerevolutionary liberty is that the weight of history stands in the way of what might be called revolutionary liberty. Since the grand revolutions of England, France, or America were supposed to better secure the liberty of the people with limited government, such an outcome is now in question for how was their freedom as grant restored by the revolutionary removal of the sovereign? For example, how could the regicides of Charles Stuart or the "blameless" Louis XVI possibly restore such freedom? Such questions are polemical but they offer a significant payoff because the responses must distinguish between one set of origins and free peoples versus another. At last, the question of origins cannot be elided with a haughty shrug or the "pragmatic" reply that the question does not matter since free peoples are obviously "present" and here to stay. Instead free peoples must now be defined in terms of their origins rather than in terms of their presence.

To even pose the question of other origins for free peoples is to place them at risk both politically and philosophically. Imagine the marching revolutionaries of England, America, or France crying up liberty only to be stopped in mid-step by their comrades and asked, "wait, which freedom are we fighting for and which not, freedom as grant or freedom as right?" Even today, schoolchildren in the free societies, reading their history textbooks, might become confused by the serious mention of their other, prerevolutionary origins. And newscasters announcing celebrations for Independence Day need to know beforehand which origins are being celebrated before they transmit that information. The risk posed by the question of origins suggests that something like hegemony is necessary for free peoples. That is, what they know of themselves must suffuse their political world. "To the extent that universality of thought guarantees freedom, freedom is defined precisely over and against all exterior influence."[1]

But if Filmer and company, with their explanation of the origins of free peoples in royal charters and grants, do not answer the central question in a recognizable manner, then that means that the other origins of free peoples remain to be clarified. Gaining such insight is, of course, the main point of this book. The study of the origins of those other free peoples can now begin in some earnest. Notably, such clarification matters precisely when their origins become an urgent question, which, until this point in the argument, has hardly been the case. In this regard the student of origins today owes at least some gratitude to Filmer and those of his provocative tradition of political thought.

Because prerevolutionary liberty is unacceptable for free peoples as they are understood today, it is not Filmer but Locke who is to be consulted on the question of their origins. Consulting with Locke is hardly new when it comes to the politics of natural liberty and the peoples that subscribe to it. Locke is the prototypical liberal thinker, that is, a political thinker of high liberty or of freedom as society's paramount political value. So far has the focus on Locke been taken with regard to the liberal, if not much of the modern politics of freedom, that one observer has decried it as "the Locke obsession."[2] To be sure, Locke is not the only thinker of modern freedom. There has also been increasing evidence that the influence of the *Two Treatises* in Locke's lifetime was not as great as once thought, due to the unlucky timing of its publication.[3] Deserved or not, Locke offers a familiar theoretical touchstone to address the origins of free peoples.

While it may be an obsession, what yet more study of Locke reveals is that he made an extraordinary effort for the origins of free peoples by ensuring that their history was similar to what is to come. Such effort is part and parcel of the origins of free peoples. Locke did not want his revolutionaries to pause in mid-stride and ask which freedom they were advancing: freedom as grant or freedom as right. He did not want English schoolchildren in history class to be unsure of their civic tradition nor, in all probability, the American public confused when hearing announcements of Independence Day celebrations. It is clear that he did not want any such confusion because Locke never did acknowledge prerevolutionary liberty even though he completed one of the most in-depth critiques of its most systematic English proponent, none other than Sir Robert Filmer. Of Locke's *Two Treatises*, Sabine states, "the first . . . was devoted to a refutation of Filmer."[4] Laski noted, the "first [treatise] is a detailed and tiresome response to the historic imagination of Sir Robert Filmer."[5]

In the *First Treatise*, Locke shrewdly erases Filmer's defense of the peoples' liberties not by criticizing it openly but by undermining the foundation for Filmer's entire politics.[6] A critical study of the basis of Filmer's political theory meant that the prerevolutionary liberty that followed from such flawed premises did not need to be addressed at all. In this regard, it is telling that the entire second half of Locke's *First Treatise* is lost. The mystery of its missing half is intriguing because, according to Laslett, it may well have contained extensive criticisms of Filmer's "constitutionalist" writings. Such writings, which must include the *Freeholder's Grand Inquest*, contain the legal details of Filmer's conception of prerevolutionary liberty. In his preface, Locke claimed that what he had written in the missing half of the *First Treatise* was never of any worth.[7] But perhaps what he meant was that he preferred not to remind anyone of prerevolutionary liberty, not even in a critique.

If the lengthy and detailed attack by Locke is any indication, free peoples in the familiar form that they are known today cannot tolerate a dissimilar history if they are to fully originate. Their history must have a similar liberty as prior (and so as students of origins we should expect them even today to work very hard to maintain their biased history). Locke's work in the *First Treatise* is a signal that their past must not be cluttered by any other modes of free life. If so, Locke enabled this chronologically fastidious people by not only saying nothing of prerevolutionary liberty but by making its basis seem nonsensical. The *First Treatise* is thus one of the most rigorous political exercises in historical erasure. By the time Locke finishes with Filmer, nothing of political worth is left behind, certainly not any idea of liberty as royal grant. This was beneficial for the origins of those other free peoples for it leaves the chronological field empty to be filled by a different history in which freedom is postulated to begin naturally, as a right, or perhaps as a self-evident truth. It can also then become more fully secured by revolution. In this regard, by minding what is imperative, the origins of free peoples proper begin to reveal themselves.

Substantiating this interpretation, however, is difficult because what I argue is the main target of Locke's attack in the *First Treatise*—specifically, Filmer's explication of political liberty as charter or grant—is never mentioned. Indeed, this interpretation suggests that Locke omitted the mention of such liberty purposefully in the *First Treatise*, which makes offering a convincing, evidenced, argument in this regard that much more difficult. But this difficulty of fixing Locke's target has perhaps always been the case for interpreters of the enigmatic *First Treatise*. For example, Tarlton argues that the *First Treatise* was a critique of an absolutist trend growing in Locke's day.[8] Tarlton quotes directly from Locke who noted once in his text that "churchmen" and royalist "flatterers" were drawing upon the writings of Filmer for the Tory cause. For Tarcov, on the other hand, Locke had to completely undermine the belief in patriarchalism, with its politics of obedience to God and fathers, in order to "protect the liberal politics from the authoritarian claims of the patriarchal family."[9] Toppling patriarchalism meant that the liberal family, although located in the private realm, could then function as the "agency of education for liberty."

Taking a somewhat different tack, Gobetti argues that Locke learned to be a better liberal thinker in the *First Treatise* by countering Filmer's pointed challenges. For example, Filmer charged that if "natural freedom" were due to everyone, then everyone would be a ruler. But this can only be anarchy "for anarchy is nothing else but a broken monarchy, where every man is his own monarch." So Locke had to find a way to defuse the problem of the ubiquity of politics. In response, Locke developed the now familiar distinction between the familial or private sphere and the public one. That liberal distinction enabled Locke to talk politically about "natural freedom" without concern over the warning that "anarchy" would result.

Finally, as a further illustration of the difficulties of interpreting Locke's enigmatic book, Mehta suggests in the *Anxiety of Freedom* that Locke's *First Treatise* promotes a psychoanalytic resolution for modern political life. Unlike Filmer, Locke could not abide by the view that individuals can be guided by ready-made prescriptions like those found in scripture. Free individuals must instead confront and adapt to the world as it is, with its inevitable anxieties, pains and disappointments. It comes as no surprise therefore that Locke singled out Filmer for criticism. Locke's "Critique of Scriptural Politics" was an attack on paternalism with its access to easy answers and ready prescriptions.[10]

What makes my reading of Locke's main target in the *First Treatise* at least as plausible as the interpretations noted above is that two additional, revolutionary theorists of natural liberty, working independently, felt compelled to develop similar attacks on Sir Robert Filmer. Locke was not the only political thinker of natural liberty to challenge Filmer in detail, which suggests that the latter's expositions on liberty presented a profound problem. Like Locke, Algernon Sidney and James Tyrrell also wrote long defenses of the natural liberty of the people that included lengthy criticisms of Filmer. It has been mostly forgotten that half of Locke's celebrated *Two Treatises of Government* matches in theme the work of other revolutionary thinkers such as Tyrrell's *Partriarcha non Monarcha* and Sidney's *Discourses Concerning Government*.[11] Schochet notes of this natural liberty triumvirate that, "[t]heir books were often page-by-page critiques of *Patriarcha* and other works, . . ."[12] For example, "Algernon Sidney, like Locke, expounded much of his political philosophy by attacking Filmer."[13] Also, "James Tyrell, Locke's friend . . . wrote a refutation of Filmer along lines similar to Locke's . . ." Of Tyrrell's *Patriarcha non Monarcha*, Laslett states, the "published book begins with a page by page refutation of *Patriarcha* in rather the same way as Locke's work in its final form begins with the *First Treatise* . . . so many of Tyrrell's positions against Filmer were also those of Locke."[14] Not only the content but the similar, grinding detail of the critiques developed by Sidney, Tyrrell, and Locke has elicited comment. For instance, Robbins echoes complaints about the *First Treatise* noting that, "Sidney examined the laws of succession [of *Patriarcha*] with a wearisome amount of illustration."[15]

Historically speaking, the dragon of Filmer had to be slain because his royalism supported a mode of freedom that ideologically confuted the possibility of the other, natural version of freedom. Filmer's now-forgotten version of freedom was not the latent, natural type, but chartered freedom that required the acquiescence and the arbitrary power of the sovereign to originate it. Restoration Whig and revolutionary theoreticians of natural liberty were comfortable with debates over royal prerogative but not royalist liberty. With the forceful response of Charles II to the Exclusion tracts and other worrying events, the Whig cause was on the defensive in the early 1680s.[16] The untimely release of the *Patriarcha* in which an erudite royalist concisely and cogently championed freedom did not help matters ideologically. The publication of Filmer's *Patriarcha* broke the Whig monopoly on talk of liberty in England's Restoration period. Hence the idiosyncratic gentleman scholar from Kent could not be left unchallenged.

Philosophically, the problem of Filmer was not simply that he had offered a better Tory defense of liberty (some Tories kept their distance from it), but that he seems to have designed it to precisely block the possibility of natural liberty. For a politics of natural liberty, the requirement of firstness is especially acute. Locke's state of nature, for example, must be humanity's *a priori*, default condition.[17] That past cannot be occupied by another, older version of the people's liberties. By systematically explicating the deepest "original" of "the rights of Englishmen," Filmer deftly occupied the philosophical and temporal space that would otherwise have been held by revolutionary theorists of the "natural liberty of the people."[18] Filmer's conception of political liberty philosophically disallowed both the Roundheads and later revolutionaries from drawing upon the ground of natural liberty for a right to resist or a right to contract limited government. Presciently, in challenging dissenters with his defense of chartered liberty, Filmer anticipated and countered the necessary chronological structure of argument for "natural liberty" that would be needed only a few decades later for a Glorious Revolution and a new Settlement.

The point of addressing Locke's *First Treatise* now is essentially as an instructive indicator that something important was at stake for the origins of free peoples. Written in the same spirit as the discourses of Sidney or Tyrrell, Locke's text signals that Filmer constituted a serious ideological, political, and philosophical problem for the kind of free peoples celebrated today. Working across generations, Sidney, Tyrell, and Locke constituted a forceful triumvirate to ensure that only one account of the history of political liberty was heard and not any other. It is a credit to the extraordinary quantity of their critical effort that Filmer is still not considered a defender of free peoples (in contrast to the abundant evidence presented in the prior chapter that he was indeed so). If anything the general view is just the opposite, namely, that Filmer is today supposed as an enemy of free peoples. Whether or not that particular criticism of Filmer was deserved, it is a tribute to Filmer's political thought that so much critical effort had to be expended against him.

Locke's First Satire

Locke's unusual refutation in the *First Treatise* consists of the repeated charge that Filmer's view of political origins is unsubstantiated. The text ends abruptly in the middle of advancing yet another such charge, as if such accusation could continue without refutation *ad infinitum*. No mention of prerevolutionary liberty is mentioned there, nor need it be if its fundamental basis is undermined. In a brief note on methodology entitled *Concerning Reading and Study*, Locke noted that, "[p]olitics contains two parts very different the one from the other, the one containing the original of societies and the rise and extent of political power, the other, the art of governing men in society."[19] With regard to his theory of political origins, "Sir Robert" is said in the *First Treatise* to be syntactically wrong, semantically wrong, methodologically wrong, historically wrong, argumentatively wrong, scripturally wrong, etc. Locke's interrogation of "origins" astutely undercuts Filmer's chartered freedom and his "art of governing men" without having to mention them. After such complete erasure, Locke can then "restore" his own version of political origins, or natural liberty, to its necessarily, primary chronological position.

Unlike Tyrrell's or Sidney's critiques, Locke's *First Treatise* is not so much an attempt to philosophically engage Filmer's political thought as to parody it. This may have been a more effective ideological strategy than grappling with Filmer constitutionally on a point-by-point basis. Instead of subtly contrasting one form of liberty with another or rationally comparing the benefits of one modality with another, Locke simply makes Filmer ridiculous as an author. The deployment of satire against an opponent in ancient rhetoric, with the Sophists for example, is well known. The deployment of satire for the origins of the free peoples in England may be said to begin not with Locke and the Glorious Revolution but with Milton and the harsher English revolution decades earlier. For example, the exaggerated imagery of Satan in Milton's *Paradise Lost* inspired the Dissenters to associate Satan with the Stuarts (although on the other hand, others associated Cromwellian failure with demonic defeat).[20]

In contrast to an emphasis on the prowess of satire in the *First Treatise*, recent observers like Tully or Ashcraft cite the philosophical weaknesses of Filmer's argument in order to "score the win" decisively to Locke.[21] Ashcraft and Tully argue that Filmer unwisely merged "natural law" thinking with "positive divine law" thereby leaving himself open to devastating criticism. However it is important to recall the dispute between Filmer and Locke not as a high-minded debate over theoretical consistency but simply between two contenders striving to undermine their opponent's most important philosophical and ideological requirements.[22] After all, the core of Sir Robert Filmer's political theory, by his own account in *The Necessity* and based upon his backhanded endorsement of Hobbes's *Leviathan*, is Bodin's theory of sovereignty. That theory remains philosophically powerful even if it was covered by a theological veneer in the work of Filmer.

In the *First Treatise*, Locke turns to the acerbic techniques of parody to achieve his critical aim of complete historical erasure. Identifying and collocating these techniques in terms of *rhetorical figures* will help to demonstrate Locke's overall method of parody.[23] For example, Locke begins with *aporia*, or by feigning doubt about the path forward by asserting the mysteriousness of Filmer's argument for "arbitrary power." "Where those *Proofs and Reasons* for Adam's Sovereignty are . . . I confess, I cannot find . . ." In the preface, even though Filmer was a quite concise writer, Locke makes exaggerated reference to the "Obscurities and Windings of . . . his [Filmer's] wonderful System." Locke then issues a broad challenge that has little to do with understanding Filmer's politics: "let him try whether he can, with all his Skill, make Sir Robert intelligible, and consistent with himself, or common sense." Once Locke leaves the preface, he repeats this *prolepsis*, or anticipation of a result, finding "nothing but a Rope of Sand."

Locke then charges Filmer with not a syntactic problem but a semantic one. Thus, "he hath not given us any Definition, or Description of Monarchy in general;"[24] Nevertheless "our A—" (Locke's reference to the author of *Patriarcha*, a *litotes* that simultaneously undermines any reference to him) has "talked so much of it." Locke's Filmer proceeds to discuss the right to fatherly authority in terms of its monarchical politics, taking it for granted that the former was understood. Of course, this is not the case since what it is that "Kings" have a right to is precisely what is at stake. In addition, according to Locke, there are only fragments of what Filmer means by fatherly authority and these lie "scatter'd" about throughout his "Writings." "He is very frequent in such Assertions," Locke notes. Then, using *parachesis*, or repetition of similar sounds as a criticism, Locke states that Filmer's terms all suggest signs of enormous political power. Thus, "the power of Life and Death . . . Adam was Lord of all . . . Kings are above the Laws . . . according to his own Will . . . Power to dispose or sell his Children . . . Power of Castrating . . . the Supremacy should be unlimited."[25] Yet Filmer has not "given any other Proofs of *Adam's Royal Authority*, other than by often repeating it, which, among some Men, goes for Argument." Such a method is unpersuasive for repetition alone will only convince "some" men to oblige themselves to an arbitrary ruler.

In the chapter of "Paternal and Regal power" Locke critically deploys *hypophora*, or raises both a question of objection and its reply, and contends that the question raised by the *Patriarcha* is whether princes have the same right as "Adam" to "Command . . . over the whole world." Locke never addresses whether this power has also enabled English liberties. Instead:

This Fatherly Authority then, or Right of fatherhood, in our A—'s sense is a Divine unalterable Right of Sovereignty, whereby a Father or a Prince hath an Absolute, Arbitrary, Unlimited and Unlimitable Power, over the Lives, Liberties and Estates of his Children and

Subjects; so that he may take or alienate their Estates, sell, castrate or use their persons as he pleases, they being all his Slaves, and he Lord or Proprietor of every Thing, and his unbounded Will their Law.[26]

Using *catachresis*, or the improper extension of meaning, Locke exaggerates the immoral implications of such authority by emphasizing not chartered liberty but that princes could have all those around them, children, wives, and servants as possessions.

Generously, Locke's "method" is to advance numerous explanations for rightful authority which is a *pleonasm* or redundant arrangement. These possibilities include the "Right" to absolute power by Eve's subjection, by paternity, by creation, by donation, by inheritance, and so on. Unfortunately, each of these justifications from Filmer has, in turn, numerous interpretations that could be drawn. For example:

I fear I have tired my Reader's Patience by dwelling longer on this Passage than the weightiness of any argument in it seems to require; but I have unavoidably been engaged in it by our A—'s way of writing, who hudling several Suppositions together, and that in doubtful and general terms, makes such a medly and confusion, that it is impossible to shew his mistakes, without examining the several Senses, wherein his Words may be taken, in any of these various Meanings, they will consist together, and have any Truth in them.[27]

What is worth noting from this passage is how Filmer's "confusion" has multiplied. Just to "shew his mistakes," Locke must address each and every possible justification that Filmer had in mind.

Locke then assists his opponent and his readers by advancing some possible explanations. "But let us see, how he [Filmer] puts his *Creation* and this *Appointment* together." In this tiny chapter, Locke proposes six different possible readings as the meaning for "Adam's Title by Creation."[28] First, if Filmer means that Adam's right to absolute power arises "by creation," that, claims Locke, would be nonsensical because then whatever God has created, say, a "Lion," for example, would thereby have the right to rule. Recognizing that this possibility is too ridiculous even for Filmer, Locke notes that Filmer did refer only to "Adam" as having "God's Appointment" to be "Governor" of the world.[29] But at the time there were no subjects around to be governed so Adam's government could not have been possible and this even "our A—here confesses."

Locke then proposes perhaps the most fascinating explanation for the right by creation: "*Monarch of the world* is also differently used by our Author, for sometimes he means by it Proprietor of all the World exclusive of the rest of mankind." But an inescapable problem of timing, or *hysteron proteron*, makes that outcome impossible for such an exclusive right cannot arise until long after the creation of Adam. If all property is to belong to Adam, exclusive of anyone else, then such a grant cannot be "spoken" until there is someone to be excluded (i.e., at least until after "Eve" had been "made and brought to" Adam). However, Eve and anyone else emerged only at a stage quite "distant in condition" from the Creation. So, in this case, Adam's right to govern cannot be based upon his sole proprietorship.

But perhaps the idea of the sovereign right through proprietorship is too detailed considering who is involved. Presumably, God does not really need to specify that Adam must be a proprietor in order to have the sovereign right. Rather, it could simply be declared that Adam has been given that right. And so Locke fixes upon another possible explanation for the right by creation. Suppose Adam was "Monarch" by a "positive Donation" because that high post was due to Adam by the "Right of Nature." But this "would always be a false Inference" since there would be no need for any positive Donation if the right was already due to Adam by "Nature."

It is also possible that what Locke's Filmer means by the right by creation is that it is a right based upon either the "Right of Nature" or the "Law of Nature." Filmer had suggested that Adam was to be governor, by a right or law of Nature, over his "posterity." Locke dismisses the possibility of having the sovereign right due to the "Right of Nature" as a mere *tautology*.[30] But if Filmer means here something like a law of nature, then this can suggest the right follows from the act of begetting such that "a Man is *by Nature Governor* of his Children." But again, the example of Adam brings with it problems of timing in that he was not yet a "Father" at the Creation. Unless, Filmer "will have him [Adam] to be a Father before he was a Father, and to have a Title before he had it."

Yet if Adam could be a father before he was a father then he might also be "a Governor without Government . . . and a King without Subjects." And perhaps then also, "Sir Robert [was] an Author before he writ his Book, not in Act tis true, but in Habit, for when he had Published it, it was due to him, by Right of Nature, to be an author, . . ." Locke's *sarcasm* here embarrasses even his sympathetic editor. Laslett notes quickly, however, that while these "paragraphs are typical of the least attractive features of Locke on Filmer, he has the grace to apologize."[31]

It could be that a sort of titular fatherhood could be exactly what Locke's Filmer had in mind. That is, suppose his patriarchal theory is metaphorical. There would then be no need to argue that the subjects of the prince are also his biological children. After all, even in a modern age of biotechnology and DNA testing this would be a difficult argument to support. Instead, a *metaphorical* rendition would have to claim only that the prince rules in a fatherly style. But even were this the case, says Locke, it sidesteps the main issue. "For the Question is not here about Adam's actual Exercise of Government, but actually having a title to be Governor."[32] How Adam, and the princes that followed him, rule is not yet the point. Filmer has forgotten to first demonstrate whether there is a right to such monarchical rule.

So having "got through the forgoing Passage, where we have been so long detain'd . . . Let us go on to his next Argument." "Adam's Title to Sovereignty by Donation" is the subject of the fourth chapter of Locke's treatise. And "our A—'s" next argument, says Locke, is that Adam was "General Lord of all things" by a "donation" from God. Almost immediately, Locke begins to develop the idea of Filmer's confusion:

> Before I examine this Argument [for Donation], and the Text on which it is founded, it is necessary to desire the Reader to observe, that our A—, according to his usual method, begins in one sense and concludes in another; he begins here with *Adam's* propriety, or *Private Dominion, by Donation;* and his conclusion is, *which shews the Title comes from Fatherhood.*[33]

This leap of logic, an *anacoluthon*, by which every premise leads to some title to absolute power, is part and parcel of what Locke calls Filmer's "usual method." Locke here also conducts *hyperbaton* by breaking Filmer's logic into three parts. Thus, it is not only (1) his "usual method" that is to be interrogated, but also (2) "this Argument" for the title by donation, as well as (3) "the Text on which it is founded."

Locke proceeds to check the case for sovereignty by donation based upon the verse (Gen. 28) that states, "and God blessed them, saying, be fruitful and multiply . . . and have Dominion over the Fish of the Sea, and over the Fowl of the Air, and over every living thing that moveth upon the Earth. From whence our A—concludes, *that Adam, having here Dominion given him over all Creatures, was thereby Monarch of the whole World.*" There is no section in Filmer's corpus where he states his argument in this disconnected fashion. Nevertheless, if Locke's "excerpt" is any indication, "our A—" is once again proceeding with his "usual" illogical "method."

So Adam is supposedly monarch of all the earth because he has been granted dominion. By dominion, Locke suggests that it is "Private Dominion" that Filmer has in mind, as in Adam possessing everything as his personal property to do with as he pleases.[34] There are two possibilities in this regard. What is owned by Adam could be either the "Earth" or the creatures roaming the world. Locke soon challenges both of these views as arguments for Adam's sovereignty. First, he does not agree that Adam had any private ownership but only that he had an ownership "in common" with all mankind. Furthermore, whatever right Adam might have over the living creatures of the earth could extend only to the "Inferior Creatures" and not to "those of his own Species."

To begin the rebuttal, Locke turns to the original "Hebrew" since, in contrast to Filmer's reading, the "Scripture itself is the best interpreter." For Laslett, editor of the Cambridge edition, this shift to the Hebrew was apparently something of a puzzle as "it adds very little to the argument." Laslett goes so far as to consult with a "Regius Professor of Hebrew" to check if he has missed something.[35] Laslett has missed nothing however, for the shift to another tongue adds little to that "argument." But it adds a great deal to Locke's critique. One effect of pointing out in Hebrew the flaws in the idea that God granted Adam dominion is to show that Filmer is a less erudite thinker, unwilling or unable to check his own primary sources that, if he had, indicate that Adam had not been donated dominion over men.

Locke's use of the Hebrew is relatively sparing but it is enough to uncover another important point. Locke explains that the disputed verse from Genesis suggests that on the fifth day God had created the fish and fowl, while by the sixth day the "the Irrational Inhabitants of the dry land" had been created. Man then had not yet been created. Locke spends some time explaining that the land-bound creatures, presumably the only "moving" creatures that Filmer could imply were human, were simply cattle, "*Wild Beasts* and *Reptils*."[36] So any dominion which was granted to Adam was only over these lesser land inhabitants. Locke thus ascribes an *ellipse* to Filmer in which a necessary logical link or term is suppressed. That is, none of the words in the disputed verse "contain in them the least appearance of anything that can be wrested, to signifie God's giving to one Man Dominion over another, *Adam* over his Posterity."

Locke is also attentive enough to the words of the disputed verse to suggest that whatever grant was donated "it was not to Adam in particular."

For "it was spoken in the Plural Number, God blessed *them*, and said unto *them* have Dominion."[37] Locke suggests that, at the very least, what God meant here is Adam plus Eve. Locke's Filmer however simply ignores the plural pronoun, having engaged in *enallage*, or the substitution of a plural form for a singular form. Thus, drawing from more excerpts of Filmer's, "God says unto *Adam* and *Eve*, Have Dominion; *thereby*, says our A., *Adam was Monarch of the World*." How inattentive of Filmer to make yet another too quick leap of logic, this time against the very words of scripture.

Charitably, Locke tries to anticipate Filmer's response to the idea that any donation from God was granted to a plural entity. "But perhaps it will be said, Eve was not made till afterward." The problem with this justification is that it will not lead to any conclusion that Filmer would want. Thus "[g]rant it so, What advantage will our A—get by it? The Text will be only the more directly against him." Given that the words of the disputed verse from Genesis state that the grant is made to "them" there is no way to construe this grant for Adam alone. At best, Locke's Filmer is left with a paradox, whereby he is correct to note that Eve has not yet been created when that grant was made but also that there was no plural "them" at the time to whom the grant could have been promised. And so, as Locke puts it, the "Text" then works against Filmer's position on Adam for there also are many other places in the Bible where God does give to "Mankind" as a whole or to the "whole Species of Mankind."[38]

In order to maintain the "Fiction and Phantasie" of the private dominion of Adam, Locke's Filmer obsessively goes so far as to "destroy the Community granted to Noah and his Sons." Where the "Text says God blessed Noah and his sons," Filmer would have this mean that only Noah received the grant for "although the Sons are there mentioned with Noah . . . it may best be understood, with a Subordination or Benediction in Succession." That is, God's blessing has built within it the understanding that only the "Father" has been granted the right. The sons too will enjoy private dominion but only after their father has passed away. This interpretation may "indeed" be "best" notes Locke, but only because it "best serves his [our A—'s] purpose."

Locke then suggests that the argument for Adam's right to sovereignty might derive from the "subjection of Eve."[39] From the dictate that "thy desire shall be to thy Husband, and he shall rule over thee. Here we have (says he) the Original Grant of Government." Locke challenges the logic of this view, for its conclusion implies a particular inconsistency, or *anacolouthon*, on

God's part. At the time when God issued this judgment against Eve, He was "declaring his Wrath against them both . . . for he [Adam] too had his share in the Fall." Therefore "we cannot suppose that this was the moment, wherein God was granting Adam Prerogatives and Privileges . . ." Indeed it would be "hard to imagine, that God, in the same Breath" would make Adam absolute monarch while condemning him to be a "day laborer for his Life." Filmer's apparent response to the fact that his "Monarch," Adam, will have to "work for his living" is a practical one, namely, that there was no other to do so. Other than Eve, there are no "Subjects . . . to work for him" and so Adam will have to fend for himself. But perhaps some time "afterwards," having lived for "900 Years," there would be enough people to do such work. Only then, finally, can Adam rest majestically on his throne.

But God did not say that Adam will have to work because of the circumstance of a lack of subjects. Rather he must do so "not only whilst thou are without other help, save thy Wife, but as long as thou livest, shalt thou live by thy Labour . . . *till thou return unto the Ground.*" Anticipating Filmer's response for him, or *prolepsis*, Locke acknowledges that "[i]t will perhaps be answered . . . that these words are not spoken Personally to Adam, but in him, as their Representative, to all Mankind." But if this is the case then God must be very hard to understand indeed. Here Locke ascribes *chiasmus*, or paired contrast to Filmer's thinking. Thus "our A—" had earlier argued that, although God spoke in the plural, He was actually speaking in the singular of patriarchs like Adam or Noah. Now, when God is speaking directly to Adam, Filmer is suggesting that he is speaking to all "Mankind."

"Farther it is to be noted, that" the disputed verse, if viewed "Whole," not only says nothing of a grant to Adam but is a statement directed primarily at Eve or women. To paraphrase, their sorrow will be multiplied in childbirth and their desire "shall be to thy Husband, and he shall rule over thee." But far from being a grant of authority over women, it is not even clear that the "weaker Sex" must be "so subjected" according to that "Curse." It is more a description of "Woman's Lot" as seen generally in the "Customs of Nations." Being merely this kind of description, or perhaps a prediction of things to come, women could someday avoid the pain of labor if there "be found a Remedy for it." As for the other part of the "Curse," any subjection which wives may be in with their "Husbands" is a matter of the particular "Circumstances of either her Condition or Contract," which, depending upon the details, could actually "exempt her from it."

But perhaps recognizing the radical, if not blasphemous, basis for interpreting God's commands as mere descriptions, Locke notes that if the "words here spoke to Eve must" be seen as a "Law" that binds women, then this is only so much subjection as "what every Wife owes her Husband . . ."[40] But how this *catachresis* can translate into a political right, asks Locke, is unfathomable. For if each wife is subject to her husband in a political sense then "there will be as many Monarchs as there are Husbands." And that would be anarchy. So if there is any subjection of women that results from God's curse then this is strictly a "Conjugal Power." And such delimited power certainly does not lead to the husband having a "Political Power of Life and Death over her, much less over anybody else."

Locke's final chapter challenging the proofs of "Adam's sovereignty" addresses whether Adam has a "natural Right of Dominion, over his Children, by being their Father." The impact such an argument has on freedom is that

> every Man that is born is so far from being free, that by his very *Birth he becomes a Subject of him that begets him*, O. 156 [232]. So that *Adam* being the only Man Created, and all ever since Being Begotten, nobody has been born free.[41]

Not having been birthed, Adam escapes the natural subjection of everyone else after him. Furthermore, Adam must come "by this Power over his Children" through the act of "begetting them." But Filmer offers no argument for his contention of the right to absolute power based upon fatherhood. "Had he been an Absolute Monarch, this way of talking might have suited well enough."[42] But like anyone else in his political theory, Filmer is merely another "subject" whom Filmer himself has "much lessen'd" in authority. And everyone knows that one "Slave's Opinion without proof is not of weight enough to dispose of the Liberty and fortunes of all Mankind." Filmer's *contradiction* here implies that since slaves are at least "equal" in their slavery, Locke could just as well oppose his own opinion to Filmer's and say that the "Begetting of Children makes them not slaves to their Fathers."[43]

Filmer's argument for patriarchal power is also morally questionable, for Locke associates the argument from fatherhood with cannibalism. Pointing out "instances of this Absolute Fatherly Power in its heights and perfection," Locke refers to old Peru where "they made their Captives their Mistresses and choisely nourished the Children they had by them, till about thirteen years old they Butcher'd and Eat them."[44] Laslett argues that this graphic quotation "has no particular relevance and seems to have been dragged in to make a sensation."[45] In this instance of *catachresis*, Locke claims to

follow the emphasis that Filmer himself places upon the absolute power of
the father. Filmer refers to nations as diverse as Persia, Upper Asia, Gaul,
and the West Indies as places where "parents have power of life and death
over their children." Filmer also spoke with approval of the "judicial law
of Moses," which allowed a father to "stone his disobedient son." Locke is
however quick to point out that even the "Dens of Lions and Nurseries of
Wolves know no such Cruelty as this . . . They will Hunt, Watch, Fight and
almost Starve for the Preservation of their Young." Such a cruel argument
could justify even "Adultery, Incest and Sodomy."

The next problem that Locke's Filmer faces with his argument from
fatherhood is that of conflicting jurisdictions. He says that, "as Adam was
Lord of his Children, so his Children had a Command and Power over
their own Children." But even granting that Adam had absolute power over
his children, his rightful authority is secure only for the "first Generation."
By the time Adam had "Grand-children" it becomes impossible to distinguish who is lord, for the grandchildren must answer to their fathers while
these same fathers must report to Adam "so that they are at the same time
Absolute Lords, and yet Vassals and Slaves."

Filmer himself acknowledges the obedience that children owe to their
parents and in the process unwittingly places his patriarchalism in another
contradiction that cannot be salvaged: "I see not then how the Children, or
of any Man else can be free from Subjection to their Parents." For Locke,
such subjection implies that no man since Adam can be absolute monarch
by the right of fatherhood since every child afterwards is a subject.[46] But
suppose Filmer means something like parents are beholden to "Absolute
Authority of their Father" and yet have "some Power over their Children."
On the one hand, this places Filmer in a new *contradiction* whereby Adam
cannot be absolute monarch, for if "the right" follows from "paternal power"
and Adam's children possess it, then Adam cannot be sovereign because the
right is not his. But once Adam's children have the sovereign right, and since
the "Subjection of Children" is the "Foundation of all Regal Authority," then
Filmer would anarchically create "as many Kings as there are Fathers."

Ultimately, it turns out that such "Absolute Natural Power, which he
[Filmer] calls Fatherhood" can be found with almost anyone. Thus Locke
intones in an end-rhyme, or *homoioteleuton*, that

> sometimes Adam alone has it all,
> Sometimes Parents have it . . . ,
> Sometimes Children during their
> Father's lifetime,

Sometimes Fathers of Families,
Sometimes Fathers indefinitely . . .[47]

The lack of a precise argument for the sovereign power is now fully documented by this point of the *First Treatise*. That Filmer's right of authority cannot be identified implies that political power could *antithetically* come into,

any hands, any how, and so by his [Filmer's] Politicks give to democracy Royal Authority, and make an usurper a Lawful Prince. And if it will do all these fine Feats, much good do our Author and all his Followers with their Omnipotent Fatherhood, which can serve for nothing but to unsettle and destroy all the Lawful Governments in the World, and to Establish in their room Disorder, Tyranny and Usurpation.[48]

Locke's critique ultimately demonstrates that Filmer's theory of political origins is unfounded, poorly conceived, contradictory, and confused. Whatever government or politics that follows from such origins, such as liberty as charter or grant, cannot be taken seriously. If, despite these flaws, it is applied anyway, then "it can serve for nothing but to unsettle and destroy all the Lawful Governments in the World."

Ramifications

With the *First Treatise*, the demise of Filmer's politics is complete without ever hearing of his prerevolutionary liberty. Yet it cannot be concluded from Locke's critique that the coming theory of the origins of free peoples based upon nature was philosophically superior to the earlier theory of origins rooted in sovereignty. That argument was never developed by Locke. In this case, more reasonable argument did not carry the day. For that argument one could find other lengthy critiques of Filmer on behalf of natural liberty that were not as satirical. Tyrrell's *Patriarcha non Monarcha* and Sidney's *Discourses Concerning Government* also could not allow Filmer's defense of freedom to go unanswered. The tone of Locke's work however is palpably caustic. Writing that extended and tiresome parody likely drew a rare grin from its taciturn author. As Laslett noted, "Locke's book is cumbersome and uninviting: two hundred unreadable pages."[49]

The other noticeable difference between the *First Treatise* and similar critiques derives from Locke's editorial discretion. Locke textually separated

his criticism of Filmer's source of political authority from his own rendition of the "original" of politics. In contrast to Tyrrell or Sidney who weave
Filmer's ideas throughout their political discourses, Locke mentions him
only once by name in the *Second Treatise*. As a result Locke clarified for
his audience a linear chronology of their political liberty as never before.
While other seventeenth-century pamphleteers waded through Restoration
debates over the English constitution and the meaning of various legal
disputes between Parliament and Crown, Locke's readers were envisioning
only the transition from the state of nature through the state of war to civil
society. On this reading of the *Two Treatises*, Locke was a kind of ideological magician, removing from sight what had otherwise cluttered their
view. Or rather, he was a better magician than those authors who muddled
the progression of origins for their readers by continually intermingling
Filmer's political theory, however critically, with their own.

Finally, the *First Treatise* also provides important practical insight into
the ideological requirements of natural liberty then and now, at least to
the extent that contemporaries today still claim to be born free, are free
by virtue of their humanity, and so forth. It is a reminder that the greatest political challenge to such freedom may not be akin to the arbitrary
power of a patriarch nor even the noxious injurers of Locke's state of war.
Subscribers to natural freedom are traditionally quite familiar with such
threats and have successfully risen institutionally and militarily to those
challenges. Instead, what can be called the clash of liberations may pose
the greatest test. In the future, the proponents of Lockean freedom and
the descendents of his political revolutions may again encounter advocates
of an extraordinary source of freedom other than natural right. The *First
Treatise* suggests that during such a clash the past is as much at stake as the
future and so opponents should challenge origins not policy and should
employ parody not philosophy.

Notes

1. Butler, "Restaging," 17.
2. Nederman, "Introduction," 23.
3. Jones, *Liberty Secured*, 49.
4. Sabine, *History*, 523.
5. Laski, *Political Thought*, 38.
6. "In the *Two Treatises*, Locke had almost nothing to say regarding the third
chapter of *Patriarcha*," Burgess, *Absolute Monarchy*, 221.
7. "Reader, thou hast here the beginning and end of a discourse concerning government; what fate has otherwise disposed of the papers that should have

filled up the middle, and were more than all the rest, it is not worthwhile to tell thee," Locke, *Two Treatises*, Preface. Suspiciously, Tyrrell also refused to address *The Freeholder's* in his critique of Filmer, claiming disingenuously, a deficiency of learning about constitutional law. See Gough, "James Tyrrell," 586.

8. Tarlton, *A Rope of Sand*, 44.

9. Tarcov, *Locke's Education*, 214.

10. Mehta, *Anxiety*, 60.

11. The theoretical traditions that support each writer in this triumvirate can be distinguished. Tyrrell is associated with the legalist-contractarian school of Grotius while Sidney's more radical theory of popular sovereignty is said to have affinities with Spinoza; Tuck, *Natural Rights*, 170.

12. Schochet, *Patriarchalism*, 193.

13. Resnick, "Locke," 102.

14. Laslett, Introduction, 60.

15. Robbins, "Algernon Sidney's," 283.

16. Beddard, "The Unexpected," 50.

17. Rudolph, *Revolution*, 20.

18. "I say, that the nations, whose rights we inherit, have ever enjoyed the liberties we claim, and always exercised them in governing themselves popularly, or by such representatives as have been instituted by themselves, from the time they were first known in the world." Sidney, *Works*, 421.

19. Locke, *The Educational*, 400–401.

20. King, *Milton*, 44–45.

21. Tully, *An Approach*, 301; Ashcraft, *Locke's Two Treatises*, 71.

22. As one Filmer sycophant put it, the question is whether the rights of Englishmen "were derived from the Laws of Natural Liberty, or from the Grace and Bounty of Princes," Bohun, *A Defence*, 5.

23. Smyth, *Greek Grammar*, 671–83.

24. Locke, *First Treatise*, §7.

25. Ibid., §9.

26. Ibid., §9.

27. Ibid., §19.

28. Ibid., §15.

29. Ibid., §16.

30. Ibid., §17.

31. Ibid., §27; Laslett, Introduction, 153; Schochet, *Patriarchalism*, 120.

32. Locke, *First Treatise*, §18.

33. Ibid., §22.

34. Ibid., §23.

35. Laslett, Introduction, 158.

36. Locke, *First Treatise*, §26.

37. Ibid., §29.

38. Ibid., §30–31.

39. Ibid., §44.

40. Ibid., §48.

41. Ibid., §50.

42. Ibid., §51.

43. Notably, this small section is the only challenge to the power of fatherhood in the *First Treatise.*

44. Locke, *First Treatise,* §57.

45. Laslett, Introduction, 182.

46. Locke, *First Treatise,* §69–70.

47. Ibid., §70.

48. Ibid.

49. Laslett, Introduction, 61.

4

A Theory of Liberation

People know what they do, they frequently know why they do what they do, but what they often don't know is what what they do does.[1]

Michel Foucault, *Madness and Civilization*

Freedom requires frenetic effort, much more than is typically understood. This chapter replicates that effort in all of its contemporary intensity thereby demonstrating the origins of free peoples. For the most part, the times now mask this frenetic activity with the "cool" interpretation of freedom as consumerism. The consumerist view, as a total system that encourages buyers and also provides them with a multiplicity of products, has gained currency of late with writers such as Bauman or Donahue.[2] But consumerism is no more liberty than is bargaining for a scarf in a Mombai market. The old slogan, "live free or die", offers a better, nontepid sense of the magnitude of effort required. But even that does not say enough if it means only the idea of fighting or warring to defend liberty. Surprisingly, that too is not activity enough; free peoples do much more than that all of the time. To put it another way, the origins of free peoples were not a grand, one-time revolutionary affair of 1688, 1776, or 1789 but an ongoing configuration of frenetic practices and effects. They include maintaining the particular history of the free peoples as well as the particular threats to them. Any lessening of intensity in their origins has a dramatic effect on what is known as a free people. Metaphorically speaking, the total effort resembles something like a loud and sustained chant that holds other concurrent chants, thoughts, or ideas at bay.[3] The twin refrain in this song of liberty is that "you have been free" and "your freedom is threatened."

Liberation: it is an all encompassing effort. For the English speaker, liberation may be the one word that can encapsulate the frenetic, ongoing experience of free peoples. In this context, to address liberation is to recall the ongoing practices and rules needed even for the free peoples. Admittedly, the term liberation is rarely applied to the 'already' free peoples, if it is called upon at all lately, because it often denotes a process for those who are not yet free. For example, it is applied to colonized peoples. One hears of a national liberation front, movement, or organization. There is also women's liberation or the women's "lib" movement. The term liberation has been attached to the liberation of animals (not their emancipation nor manumission). There is also liberation theology, which involves a change in consciousness toward the plight of the poor. The contrast between these various applications and the initial, definitive, refusal of the term seems clear. Free peoples are not to be liberated (unless, as Marcuse has it, they are trapped in the hegemonic and "biological" web of the market and technology); only unfree groups or mindsets can be liberated. This familiar differentiation in the denotation or perception of the meaning of liberation recalls Nietzsche's cryptic point in *Twilight of the Idols* about the difference between laudable, liberal strivings versus the stultification of liberal institutions.[4] The free peoples have so forgotten their origins that they can hardly imagine liberation anymore. Nevertheless there is no other single word that restates in practical terms the meaning of the origins of free peoples. To apply liberation to the free peoples despite the aforementioned connotations thus stands as a measure of how much rethinking is necessary. At least analytically, the student of origins proceeds as if the free peoples start on their way to freedom every morning; "freedom always appears as a movement of liberation."[5]

Locke's *Two Treatises of Government* is a familiar reminder of the tremendous actions or liberation that must be taken for free peoples. Specialists and historians of political thought often complain that Locke did not establish his political views within the theoretical currents of the day.[6] That was not simply because his singular genius fashioned new premises but because the sort of peoples he advocated and the future of their sort of freedom could not advance otherwise. The kind of peoples he foresaw were not possible had he complicated their history and origins with other views then raging in the debates over England's ancient constitution. As has been noted, Locke's *First Treatise* was a concentrated critique that left uncluttered the history,–or as Locke put it, the "original"—of the people's liberties. The *Second Treatise*, with its entirely novel history referencing their natural right, shows that Locke had to be not only critical but also creative. To boldly step forth, to wipe the past clean, and to even replace it with their own chronology remains a central part of that experience, although the free peoples no longer feel the wrenching sensation as acutely when they comfortably read their history textbooks today.

Along the way, however, free peoples were diverted by the logic of reason and that has confused how they are perceived, even by themselves, thanks in no small measure to their philosophers. To be fair, the latter are quite helpful as focused exponents of their favorite value but they also hide the main point. It is as if modern philosophers of freedom have been part of a longstanding conspiracy to downplay most of the effort to be free, in the same way that the origins have been downplayed. One's freedom, they will say, is *a priori* or already around, perhaps naturally or as an intuition. Free people therefore need only to clarify and optimize what they already know or possess. The path to such coherence or consistency is to note precisely how each threat to their freedom affects it. If I begin with the premise that I am free but know not exactly how or why, having my axiomatic state threatened is one way to advance from uncertainty and secure the matter of my paramount value. On this logic, threats to freedom are vital for that is how freedom advances more fully, or as Benn and Swanton put it, more consistently and coherently.

Not only has the concept of freedom become caught up in the philosophers' schemes of reason, but so too have the free peoples, and not without some disservice to them. The classic example is that of Hegel in which absolute freedom, to be politically grounded in a constitutionally limited monarchy, is both the guiding motivation and the truth of human reason. Kojeve's focus on the master–slave relation in the *Phenomenology of Spirit* is the most oft cited example.[7] Through his labor the slave comes to recognize that he is more than a guided object, and with his revolt the master eventually comes to see the same additional quality in the slave. Both take a step closer to absolute freedom by overcoming their one-sided perspectives through what they learned from their interactions. As they and their societies grow and mature, they eventually know something of reason actualized politically in freedom. Not to be outdone in relating freedom to the progress of reason, Fukuyama claims that all peoples now have no other option but to be free.[8] Having tried out all other political forms and experimented with various modern ideologies, freedom is all that remains, expressed politically in the form of liberal democracy. To be the kind of people that finds their paramount political value in freedom is therefore not only the tested, smart option but the "last" one.

But if anything, freedom is about fears and triumphs not progress and rationality. It is less a matter of minds than of hearts, of *soma* rather than *gnosis*. Again Locke knew this well. Most interpreters of Locke overlook his political role as a conspirator rather than as a rationalist (Ashcraft being an exception[9]). It has been mostly forgotten that Locke risked his life against

Tories who advocated a different source of the liberties of the people and had the force of the Crown and its agents to support them. In his *Two Treatises* Locke was not trying to polish his political conception coherently or consistently. It is merely one interpretation of Locke's political theory, offered to thousands of undergraduates yearly, that to choose his "civil society" is smarter than remaining with the "inconveniences" encountered in the natural state. This perception of freedom's rationality has been highlighted most recently by the Rawlsian thinkers of liberty, to be addressed in this chapter.

If freedom is liberation, however, and therefore that all-out, all-encompassing effort suggested above, then the contemporary philosophers of freedom are not writing of freedom or about it but *for it*. This latter effort requires more energy than the former since to struggle for something or to advocate means, at least implicitly, to counter the other, fearful possibility that it may not happen. To avoid that possibility, they must, like Locke, ensure only the specific past of their free peoples. And again like Locke, they must also produce and refine the present threats to them. Both free peoples and the philosophers who carefully express their paramount value must continually work in these ways because there are other histories and other threats that could become salient instead, especially in today's interconnected world. True, the free peoples as they are known today do not start from scratch as they did in Locke's day. But their particular sort of political life must still be sustained against other possibilities. Huntington's *Who are We?* offers insight into the fearful outlook that comes from not getting the beginnings of free peoples "just right." [10] Fear of diluting what Huntington calls the "American creed" is why he objects to deconstruction, immigration, and transnational elites. That creed includes, for example, individualism as a societal ideal and the Protestant work ethic. However, graduate programs in "ethnic studies" deconstruct that America because they not only do not acknowledge its creed but construct identities and histories that upend it into a story of oppression. Coupled with the newest group of linguistically resistant immigrants, who are also not beholden to the creed, Huntington worries for the future of the American venture (ominously, he finds in the prosecution of foreign threats, or what I call the practice of indictment, a means to revitalize that identity).

As contemporary liberators rather than as contemporary reasoners, Benn, Swanton, and similarly focused writers produce again the history and the threat that are particular to their free peoples and not any other possible histories or threats. Like Locke long ago, they construct the effects needed for free peoples. If they did otherwise, and if their society as a whole followed suit, they would collapse as a free people. The end of the free peoples rests in their *own* origins and energies and not in some grand scheme of reason. And like the priests of some mature religion, Benn and Swanton do their part to sustain its memory and its sensibilities among its acolytes, but not in the way they believe. The coherence of freedom was no more reason for its success in seventeenth-century England than it would be in the England of the twenty-first century. One must, rather, exclaim furiously and inscribe frenetically both the history of free peoples and the threats to them. For our part, by simply repeating what they say for free peoples, the student of origins contributes once again to their liberation.

Benn: Proto-freedom

As the title suggests, Benn's *A Theory of Freedom* is modeled after Rawls' pivotal work on justice. But instead of an original position, Benn's starting point is the underdeveloped, "natural personality" that, despite five chapters delineating the concept, looks just like the Lockean individual in that famous and near-perfect state of freedom. At one point even Benn admits the resemblance:

> Society for the liberal is compounded of natural persons, each a self-governing chooser, responsible for what he does to others and for what he makes of himself. Locke attributed to him natural rights, which might be interpreted as normative capacities that a person possesses by virtue of his natural capacity as a chooser, and on account of his commitment to making his own way . . . in a fluid and contractual society.[11]

The natural person, as the inhabitant of Benn's initial, "contractual" situation, is a chooser who pursues his or her own projects. Benn "envisages" humans as already formed choosers with interests to defend.[12] But Benn emphasizes here that this quality is not because of the grant of some right. It is more simply a function of one's natural or inherent capacity. Indeed, as will be seen, to talk about natural persons is to talk about the human species.

Benn begins delineating his initial situation, like Rawls, with a critique of utilitarianism. In the process, Benn contrasts his view of free practices as based not upon desires or preferences but upon belief structures. The "natural person" acts rather than reacts; he causes instead of being acted upon. Benn argues against the Humean idea of a sense-receiving mind with its decaying mental events.[13] On this model, often known as "no want no reason," Hume suggested that the mind depends upon a world of sense impressions that generate desires. Reason then swings into action as a means to satisfy the wants that come from sensing the world, a world that includes the body and the appetitive drives. Once satisfied, the associated mental event quickly fades away.

But for Benn, human reason is not dependent upon the "world." Instead, and more boldly, "the mind orders" the "noumenon" or the "raw stuff out there." People are, he declares, a "practically" rational "species." On this view of rationality, the "action commitments" of natural persons do not rely on want-based reason but upon beliefs grasped as true. These beliefs make up a belief system, which is one's reasoned ranking of commitments. In contrast to the Humean person who reasons according to an endless stream of wants and impressions, Benn's natural person "is committed" to act consistently with what is believed. For instance, if Helen asks Alan whether or not it is Tuesday, Alan's belief that it is Tuesday commits him to say that it is Tuesday and not some other day. It should be noted that this is not the point at which Benn's view is to be tested if Alan declares to Helen that it is Wednesday. The criteria by which that lie may be gauged have yet to be developed. Such a lapse turns out to be a serious problem. That Alan violates the rule of "consistency" indicates a defect of his rationality.

The problem at this point in Benn's scheme is that the example of Alan and Helen does not say all that much about how decisions are rendered. It does not say how natural persons figure out what to do or choose. That is a process of scanning for options, imagining their actualization, filling in the details, and developing the act commitment.[14] It is a voyage of "discovery" (a term that Raz, another contemporary thinker of freedom, also uses; Swanton prefers the somewhat less romantic word progress) that carries the natural person from what he is to what he will be. To an extent, as Benn and similar thinkers argue, his practical rationality gives him the ability to advance himself. Of course, such a prediction may also offer valuable clues for the student of origins.

To more fully develop his concept of the natural personality, Benn draws upon Hare's distinction between our everyday and "critical" reason. The former process may be almost habitual. And that is fine so far as being rational goes. There is nothing irrational about habitually making for the door "to exit" a room instead of heading toward "a wall." But critical thinking happens when we are forced to extend our belief structure in a new situation. Should a soldier on watch shoot a child walking straight toward his post? How does Agamemmnon choose between either sacrificing his daughter Iphigenia or his army? In both examples, Benn suggests that the agents already have the resources to make these extraordinarily difficult decisions. All that is needed is an extension of their "role-fulfillment curves" into new, unexplored regions. They will have to, says Benn, do some of their own moral "work." Doing so adds "inches to" one's "stature as a rational decision-maker."[15] Perhaps too something of the full origins of free peoples emerges with such extension.

The point that I would highlight, and which Benn celebrates, is that the resources for choosing, and for freedom to come, are already around to be extended. In other words, Benn's persons are protofree, a bit free already and destined for more. Thus,

> I have used the phrase, "to discover how to extend or connect up his value/principle/role-fulfillment curves" to suggest that there are both cues and constraints already within a person's belief structure suggesting how the restructuring is to be done. For such dilemmas [like that faced by Agamemnon] never exhaust our moral resources.[16]

As mentioned in my Introduction, accounts of the origins of free peoples always begin with some form of protofreedom. Some bit of freedom, the basic resources for it, are projected as already available or ready at hand. This is why Benn refers with great approval to R. Dworkin's Hercules, an ideal judicial reasoner who can draw upon "immense resources" and precedent.[17] The immensity of available resources means that they are already accessible to one for the task of improvement or progress. The natural person has this capacity and so can eventually advance to Benn's "ideal" of "freedom as autonomy." Benn is fond of saying that, in our fast-changing technological world, it is the "natural person" who can adapt well.[18] This is because he possesses the intrinsic capacity to scan, plan, and to choose. However confusing the world may be, the natural person already has the resources to order and manipulate it.[19]

What the conception of the natural personality offers to the study of free peoples is a detailed contemporary demonstration of one major factor in their origins. Just as Locke devoted a number of chapters to the natural state and the rules governing liberty therein, Benn devotes some five chapters to it. In both cases, the postulation of an initial state of freedom is a specialized synecdoche that enables the full-scale advancement of liberty or what Benn will call autarchy. Admittedly, Benn's postulation of protofreedom is only a single effort. Add to it the publication of history books, the delivery of college lectures, primary education in civics and social studies, politicians' speeches, and displays in national museums all positing protofreedom at the same time, and the effect is enormous. Benn's natural personality is a philosophical expression of protofreedom for the origins of free peoples. Projected as the starting point for free peoples, protofreedom is the premise of liberty as their natural state. Benn's conception helps bring liberty to life, for it can indicate, given the beliefs, interactions, and expectations of the "natural person," why this or that event in the life of such a person is freedom and not something else. Benn's natural personality is thus set as a standard that, although underformulated, has just enough meat on it to build up arguments about it.[20] In that way, the postulation of a part allows for the eventual understanding, discovery, or the origin of the whole.

Pronouncing the natural personality, saying that it has familiar characteristics, and postulating that it is the most basic human form is a crucial synecdoche that enables the history and advancement of Benn's sort of freedom. By positing the "core" element of what humans are, as their underdeveloped essence, so to speak, or better, as their yet-to-be-developed essence, the past of freedom is produced. And since a people (now) have this history, since their past has been posited backwards (in time, in thinking, in writing, or in politics; it becomes difficult to distinguish), it will become possible to talk about their present and future. To put it differently, thanks to a synecdoche of freedom, free peoples can then originate. In Benn's terms, without freedom's undeveloped, natural phase it would not be possible for him to later talk about its advancement from "autarchy" to full "autonomy."

The political and social problem of freedom arises when natural persons interact. It is not that natural persons are so egoistic that they will rudely pursue interests in ways that are hostile to each other. Like all of the contemporary authors in question here, Benn rejects Hobbesian liberalism, such as it is. Rather, as Locke might also have it, part of what it means to be a natural person is that there is "respect" for the status of other natural persons as planners. What it means to be a natural person is also to be moral; that is, to be considerate of the freedom of others.[21] Benn states:

> The model of personal interaction I have taken as a standard postulates individuals pursuing their own projects . . . given his structure of beliefs and values. Sometimes they compete . . . but each is committed to abstaining from doing to others what he would consider he had reason to resent their doing to himself.[22]

It would behoove the meaning and value of the natural person if such a planner, chooser, and causer did not also recognize the value that capacity holds for others. For that would mean that individual was a kind of solipsist who pursued projects, probably "bizarre" ones, which took account of no one else.

At this point, Benn cannot resist talking about threats to the natural personality and this is because it cannot advance conceptually otherwise. For Benn, freedom originates because of its usefulness and this quality becomes apparent against solipsism and a host of other deficiencies of freedom. Benn's full definition of freedom now begins to take shape or to fully originate in contrast with its deficiencies or threats. Thus:

> The concept of freedom is most at home in formulating complaints and grievances, in claiming rights [defined as normative resources one can deploy that forbear upon others] and demanding consideration of one's interests.[23]

As Benn defines it, "[t]he free agent Alan is free to φ in relation to some possible frustrating condition F." Freedom comes into view clearly only against a threat to freedom.[24] Then its usefulness or its value for "one's interests" becomes evident. Indeed, except for his introductory chapter, I do not think Benn even uses the word freedom in *A Theory of Freedom* until he introduces the threat of unfreedom in Chapter 7.

At last, with the introduction of the problem of unfreedom, Benn ends his discussion of the natural personality to talk explicitly of freedom or "autarchy." Free people fully originate, so to speak, with the first hint of unfreedom. What the natural personality means in political or social terms that involve interaction with others is "autarchy." Thus:

> Autarchy is a condition of human normality, both in the statistical sense, that the overwhelming majority of human beings satisfy it, and in the further sense that anyone who does not satisfy it falls short in some degree as a human being.[25]

Thanks to the latter caveat, which introduces degrees of autarchy or freeness, this condition can apply cross-historically, cross-culturally, and even across religions. Autarchy is strongly normative. On the surface, in cases ranging from ancient "Sparta," to some "primitive tribal cultures," to certain "religious" communities, autarchy may not seem to be the order of the day.[26] But this impression is only because they have not fully emphasized it. They did not know of their freedom but it was there all along.

If the concept of autarchy still seems somewhat sparsely developed, this is no mistake. Something rather strange happens at this point in the origins of free peoples. A kind of negative, reverse thinking is brought to bear at such moments in the account, for it is only after the identification of its threats that their freedom can be fully discerned. Benn admits:

> No term in common use corresponds precisely to the concept autarchy, perhaps because we rarely need it. For ordinary practical purposes we know well enough what a normal person is like . . . For practical, nontechnical purposes we are more likely to be in need of precise ways of identifying and differentiating deviations from the norm rather than of an accurate formulation of its criteria.[27]

For Benn, the lack of a "common" term for autarchy is because persons are, in varying degrees, already autarchic and so that knowledge can be taken for granted. But in terms of origins, the practical reason that autarchy cannot be defined is certainly not because persons already know what it means, more or less. The claim that persons are already partially anything is a synecdoche, and that they are already autarchic, if only nontechnically, is a synecdoche of freedom. Benn's lengthy underformulation is no casual discussion but a thoroughly deliberate effect and is entirely necessary for the origins of free peoples.

Benn: Anti-freedom

Let it be agreed with Benn that freedom comes alive or is "most at home" under conditions of duress. The only catch is that his freedom was not around already, naturally, or in rudimentary form, only to become more solidified, or more at home when pressing "grievances." And so too are naturally free persons in their condition of "autarchy" not simply already around. Just as Benn postulates them, and the student of origins follows in turn, so also are the protofree posited in the writing of history schoolbooks, in national museum displays, in independence celebrations, and in media reiterations. Indeed, a veritable barrage of synecdoche fills free societies and reminds members of their central political heritage. Benn's contribution in this regard is simply more elaborate or thorough than most. As a philosopher he tries to methodically cover all the bases in a book whereas on the massive scale of a free society all the bases are covered by the sheer volume of the same activity. Either way, one effect of the origins of free peoples is now demonstrated. Their freedom is not natural, intuitive, nor self-evident but depends upon the all-too-human and quite identifiable and replicable practice of synecdoche.

What this practical insight into the origins of free peoples means politically and morally is that natural liberty does not provide a criterion for the judgment of threats to freedom such as terrorism or "solipsism." Natural freedom or autarchy no longer has the status of already being around beforehand to serve as a norm to judge what happens next. Yes, Benn's "norm" should still be recognized but as protofreedom and so as the effect of the synecdoche that postulates it. As for the charge of "solipsism" as unfreedom, that too has simply been leveled. In the study of origins, such accusatory practice turns out to be crucial. As will be noted next, there are many such charges and many such attributions in *A Theory of Freedom*. But unlike Benn's argument for the usefulness of freedom in contrast to unfreedom, my claim is that the origins of free peoples depend upon the two simple but forceful practices of synecdoche and indictment. Benn's discussion of the natural person and autarchy illustrates a synecdoche of protofreedom and thus its origins. However it says nothing yet of the origins of antifreedom. The cry of unfreedom alone is a broad charge, too broad to be sure how to respond. So it has to be classified, refined, and its impacts upon freedom spelled out. Only then can it be ascertained that that unfreedom, and not some other one, is the "solipsist" type.

"Paranoiac": he "allows no one's testimony to count as evidence against his strange beliefs, even if that forces him to impugn the reliability of everyone he meets and to believe that all are in league against him." When he does encounter instances of counterevidence, he develops an endless "series of ad hoc hypotheses" to explain them away. There is nothing wrong with adjusting one's hypotheses nor even with developing new ones, say, because the evidence contradicts you. But no "scientist" would jettison a hypothesis because the experiment only worked 99 out of 100 times. Thus, while the paranoiac is in an anxious position, the acts to which he is committed do not alleviate that anxiety but foster and even heighten it. He is caught in a "self-reinforcing circle." The problem is not that the "paranoid psychotic" has no beliefs, nor is it that those beliefs do not guide action. "The essential defect of the paranoiac is that, though his theory does provide him with a map of the world, and is action guiding, it is not truth oriented." An "interpersonal" comparison of evidence is impossible.[28]

"Kleptomaniac" and the obsessive-compulsive: the kleptomaniac has "no beliefs—at least on the conscious level—that commit him to steal." He may not decide to steal or he may even decide not to steal—yet "steal all the same." Similarly, a compulsive hand washer cannot be "persuaded" not to wash his hands, that they are already clean because he has just washed them. He may know this and even recognize the "dissonance" involved between knowing that his hands are still clean and the fact that he is washing them again minutes later. The relation between his beliefs and actions is therefore very tenuous. And any "reasons" that he gives for his hand washing are out of order for they would be "posterior to the neurotic impulse to action, instead of being the action commitments of prior beliefs."[29]

"Schizophrenic," catatonic, split personality: the schizophrenic "lacks" the self-awareness of being an agent or a causer of "changes in the world." He may recognize the meaning of the conception of agency. But he does not apply that conception to himself. Instead he thinks of "himself as process or as something to which things happen." He may even "act out" this "self-conception" going so far as "catatonic paralysis, becoming for the world too the mere object he believes himself to be." In the case of "dissociation," there is a "surrender of the awareness of a continuous self." To evade some deep guilt, one persona can blame another. Alternatively, the "agent may talk as though there were different persons inhabiting and quarreling over his body."[30]

"Psychopath": the "case of the psychopath is more problematic." Although it may be classified as yet another kind of defect, "to some it is not a defect of autarchy at all but a case of wickedness, that is, of a wholly autarchic person with wholly corrupt beliefs" for action. Nevertheless there is one defect that can be confirmed in this case. It is the inability to see "any but the most immediate consequences of action as relevant considerations for decision-making." It is not that the psychopath is unaware of the long-term consequences that often ensue from his kind of actions, even when those consequences are likely and harmful to himself.[31] Although he may be highly intelligent, long-term considerations simply do not go into what often seem to be the psychopath's exceedingly rigorous calculations. Where the akratic sees the "attractive option" as a mere temptation, the psychopath finds it the "course to choose." The problem of psychopathy can be characterized as "a kind of psychic discontinuity."[32] His future self is likely to be incarcerated or, at best, beset again by the same suffering that drove him to revise his action-commitments the first time. It is not simply that he is "imprudent" but rather that the "being" who is enjoying pleasure now is never seen as connected to the one who will be suffering again in a week.

Benn: Full Freedom

Finally, Benn's free people fully originate thanks to a slew of charges of antifreedom. It must happen so, for there is no prior standard that the various "defectives" are judged against. So, for example, the "schizophrenic" is charged as antifree via an accusatory practice that posits such defectives. That full freedom is the effect of such origins is stated explicitly and, as will be illustrated, follows point by point from Benn's "discussion" of deviance. "The following requirements for autarchy emerge from this discussion of disqualifying conditions."[33] That "discussion of disqualifying conditions" ranging from schizophrenia to psychopathy has just been reiterated. Now, listed in exactly the same order as Benn has them but framed succinctly here, the "requirements for autarchy" emerge as:

(1) One person, "displaying continuity" of belief structure must be identifiable. He cannot be a schizophrenic.
(2) Whatever "the subject's other aims . . . they must be tied to a concern for truth" as a regulating idea. He cannot be a paranoid psychotic.
(3) The subject must be aware of the "action commitments of his beliefs" and be "disposed" to act according to them. He cannot be an obsessive-compulsive.
(4) The subject must be such that changes in his beliefs "must be capable of effecting changes in his practical decisions." He cannot be an obsessive compulsive or a psychopath.
(5) "The subject's belief structure must yield a ranking of action commitments" that do not lend "lexical priority" to the "immediacy of an expected gratification." He cannot be a psychopath.
(6) The subject must be capable of project-making, of "forming now an intention to act for the sake of a preferred future state." He cannot be any of the above defectives.

Freedom as "autarchy" has now fully originated.[34] It has become known in its characteristics and implications to even its previously puzzled author who just before knew it only "well enough." But the production of pro-tofreedom and antifreedom were the keys to the full emergence of his freedom, not any recognition of its usefulness. In his touching foreword to *A Theory of Freedom*, Benn recalls that his book began decades earlier as a work on "power." "Having narrowly escaped being sucked into that morass," he went on to develop his ideas on freedom. But as it turns out, that "morass," or something like it, constitutes the very key to Benn's freedom. On my reading, the origins of freedom have nothing to do with its usefulness; that is, it is not in contrast to worrisome defects of freedom that freedom itself is better recognized as useful. Rather, "freedom as autarchy" originates by producing the "natural personality," or the protofree, *and* by producing "deviance," or the antifree. Only after having developed the "deviations from autarchy" did it become possible to more fully know autarchy; that is, only then do free persons fully originate through what might be called the special powers of liberation.

For the task of distilling origins, a wrong perception has been righted. The standard account of origins has been that free peoples emerged more fully because their freedom was valuable or useful to them. This quality of freedom becomes especially clear in their encounters with threats or "defects of freedom." For example, the value of one's initially hazy freedom or the natural personality is clarified because it is more useful than psychosis. And on the grand scale of a revolution, one's natural liberty is certified as valuable when contrasted against tyranny. Whether philosophical or political, however, my reading suggests that freedom fully originates after the production of the "norm of freedom" and after the production of what "deviates" from that norm. In the cases of Locke and Benn, this practical rendition of origins emerges when their presumption that a bit of similar freedom was already prior is blocked. It was blocked historically in Locke's case by recalling the dissimilar royalist liberty as prior instead of Locke's "state of nature." It was blocked performatively in Benn's case by positing his "natural personality" so that it was not obviously natural or "normative" but produced as such through his synecdoche. Thus Benn's sort of free people are the product of replicable practices. The usefulness of freedom never comes into play on this reading for there is only synecdoche, which posits a partial version of freedom as prior, and indictment, which is the charge of antifreedom and its refinement.

With some exasperation it may now be asked, 'but is it not obvious that freedom is more valuable or useful than psychosis and schizophrenia?' The answer is that "freedom" seems more useful (or more valuable, reasonable, or normal) only so long as its origins continue to be deployed frenetically. After all, defining freedom remains notoriously difficult and so to say that "freedom" is more useful than schizophrenia is to say only that *not* being schizophrenic is a useful state. Recall that Benn's most basic definition of freedom, the natural personality, is little more than the assertion that people are choosers. His slightly stronger, political notion of freedom as autarchy was the injunction that individuals should respect the same capacity to choose in others (a norm also postulated by Locke for his state of nature). Either way, whether Benn's freedom begins philosophically with the natural personality or politically as autarchy, it depends upon the identifiable and replicable practice of synecdoche. The oft proclaimed usefulness of freedom is not a property of freedom *per se* and so is not a reason for its progress but an *effect* of the origins of free peoples, which continuously construct both protofreedom and antifreedom.

Swanton: Introduction

Two aspects of Swanton's *Freedom* stand out strongly for the study of the origins of free peoples. First, Swanton's award-winning text is even more focused than Benn' book. Swanton addresses the coherence of freedom and only that, refusing even to consider higher levels or ideals of freedom. For example, she indicates no enthusiasm for some "perfectionist" level of freedom such as Benn's notion of "autonomy" or Raz's "morality of freedom" (neither superconception discussed here). To be sure there is "progress," but it is strictly advancement in better understanding freedom not further progress to a select proficiency of freedom. Since free peoples are defined here as those fascinated peoples that claim freedom as their paramount value (in contrast to other possible aims such as justice or equality), Swanton's strong emphasis promises further insights into the origins and political life of those who have the same focus.[35]

Second, and in anticipation of the origins of free peoples, Swanton's work places extraordinary emphasis upon the identification of problems, defects, or "flaws" of freedom. Where Benn devotes only a few pages to that harsh indictment procedure, Swanton (Chapters 7–12) dedicates nearly half of her book to it. This concern with threats has not diminished in the years since the publication of Swanton's *Freedom*. As will be noted in the final chapter of *The Origins of Free Peoples*, the total liberation process has become even more ferocious of late, counting not only threats to freedom that are identified today but also future threats that could arise tomorrow.

The overall scheme of *Freedom* should not be unfamiliar to contemporary political theorists. Like Rawls, Swanton draws upon an original position that she calls the "background theory."[36] And like the original position, this "background theory of freedom" is posited as a hypothesis that is also "empirically" based. Swanton also develops the main point of our basic considerations, although of course they are our considerations of freedom rather than justice. To do so, Swanton deploys a mode of "reflective equilibrium" in order to contrast these basic considerations against instances of unfreedom. In one respect, Swanton exceeds the detail that one expects from *A Theory of Justice*. She does not simply presume and draw upon our "considerations" of the matter at hand.[37] Swanton has the list of the 23 of them![38] The following is a sample: "1. One cannot be unfree to do what one in fact does. 2. In New Zealand one was until recently unfree to commit sodomy. 3. The highway robber who utters a credible threat, 'Your money or your life,' renders you unfree in that situation." These and other basic "considerations" on freedom are culled from ordinary language usage and from views found in scholarship. They are the "endoxa" of freedom, or what "Aristotle" would call the "opinions of the wise and the many" regarding freedom.[39]

Swanton begins her analysis with the presumption of a rather garrulous free people. They are free as evidenced both by their endoxa (which are deemed to be references to their liberty) and their various "favored," if contested, conceptions of freedom (which are supported by only selected endoxa). So people are talking of their freedom, that much is clear. But that is about as far as it goes in terms of clear conceptualization. The exact nature of their freedom is not coherent, which is the problem Swanton sets out to rectify. The contemporary condition of freedom can be summed up as the "essential contestedness of freedom"; that is, there is a great deal of disagreement about the definition of freedom. Swanton therefore offers a more "coherent" conception of freedom. Of course how freedom originates or originates more fully is not so much a question of coherence but of practices and actions. Freedom may or may not ultimately be coherent, but how that fascinating value fully originates necessarily takes practical precedence.

Swanton: Proto-freedom

Protofreedom is effective only if it is posited in such a way that it enables the advancement of free peoples. It therefore has to be construed as kindred, prior, and lesser than the freedom that is to come (whether via revolution or philosophical analysis). In this case, protofreedom begins as "defeasible freedom," which is Swanton's characterization of the "background theory." According to Swanton, in order to get to this conception of the background theory, strict criteria have to be met. In this section, it is demonstrated how the delineation of these criteria constitutes Swanton's synecdoche of protofreedom. Defeasible freedom winds up being the bit of freedom in the "background" that becomes subject to fuller or more coherent clarification.

The first condition of the "background theory of freedom" is for it to be "independently satisfying."[40] It is what everyone free already knows of their liberty or, in Swanton's parlance, it must be acceptable to all concerned with freedom yet stand on it own as a different conception. On the one hand, if the background theory is to get around the frustrating problem of essential contestedness it will have to be widely acceptable. So it has to agree with all of the endoxa of freedom. But on the other hand, the background theory must be independent. It cannot be any one of those "favored" definitions of freedom that have been found in the circumstance of essential contestedness for it is conceded that no consensus is forthcoming in that contest (which is why one must turn "back" to the deepest preconceptions or endoxa of freedom for a chance at progress and coherence).

For the satisfaction requirement of a background theory, Swanton sets a number of criteria that, she argues, defeasible freedom meets better than any other theory. The first is that any "background theory" must preserve as many of the endoxa as possible; that is, unlike other conceptions, it should appeal "widely" to the endoxa. Thus, "the background theory is tailored for the accommodation of as wide a range of endoxa as possible."[41] Second, the background theory of freedom must preserve the "reasonableness" of the various endoxa. That is, it must "preserve" their "point." By meeting the condition that the background theory is widely accommodating, it is thereby possible to say that it is satisfying. Defeasible freedom is so accommodating of the endoxa that it can be classified as a conception that is satisfying to all free people or is similar to what they think of their freedom (albeit vaguely). It is also familiar since the endoxa are simply everyone's (i.e., of the "wise and the many") basic considerations of freedom.

Swanton's background theory will allow for her freedom to more fully emerge because protofreedom has been postulated. Without the background theory, no relation between this initial and a later, "coherent" instance of freedom would be ascertainable. And without such a relation no "progress" to more of the same freedom or "coherence" would be possible. When the initial postulate of freedom is so helpful in this way it can be called proto-freedom. The background theory can be pronounced as related to what is believed of freedom because it accommodates almost all of the endoxa. And it can be pronounced as related to the basis of freedom because it collocates the endoxa of freedom (which are the raw and "initial characterizations of the F phenomena." For example, the endoxa were the intuitions supporting the various contested definitions).

If the development of the background theory is a synecdoche, then it must posit the part that enables the understanding of a whole. Swanton's background theory meets that criteria as it can be characterized as the incomplete version of full-scale, "coherent" freedom. After all, it is only a collocation of the "raw" endoxa and not any fully considered view of freedom. In the discussion of Benn's "natural personality" it was noted that while that conception was somewhat indefinite it had enough meat on it to develop further arguments about it. Similarly, Swanton declares that,

> Austin's defeasibility conception of freedom serves admirably as the basis of the background theory. The idea that freedom connotes the absence of a wide variety of limitations in the practical process . . . shows promise of permitting a wide range of endoxa. Although Austin's conception provides the bones of our theory it cannot provide the meat. There is not yet enough substance to govern the way coherence is to be achieved . . . There are all kinds of flaws in the practical process, not all of which bear on freedom.[42]

Defeasible freedom is about the most underformulated starting point for origins possible as it is only "constituted by absences." For such freedom to more fully or coherently originate what limits or threatens it must certainly bear upon it. Thus the flaws "which limit a human being's potential in her role as agent . . . imparts substance to this structure."[43] Imagine, briefly, the outlook of a being who subscribes to such freedom. Such an entity would be inherently wary since unfreedom or threats must seem far more real than its own defeasible foundation.

As a further illustration of its synecdochal effect, as the part that enables understanding of the whole, Swanton notes that defeasible freedom is not to be thought of in terms of "presences." Indeed, Swanton does not hesitate to expound upon this most hazy first freedom, which is "constituted by the absence of breakdowns." Thus,

> [t]he freedom-standards to be met by the successful act are not to be described as *presences* of items (introspectible or otherwise) that *cause* bona fide free action . . . Rather, they are to be described as *absences*, viz., the absence of breakdowns of radically different kinds which afflict the different parts of the machinery of the act, (*op cit.*, p. 180). For Austin, "like 'real,' 'free' is used only to rule out the suggestion of some or all of its recognized antitheses" (*op cit.*, p. 180). In short, it is "unfree" "which wears the trousers": "free" merely signals the *absence* of all, or some, typical breakdowns besetting practical activity.[44]

A number of critics, some dubbed communitarians, have challenged such a negative conceptualization for not offering specific, social ideals for free action.[45] And if Swanton's limited conception were not provocative enough, her negative dialectic holds for unfreedom too since, according to Swanton, there is "no way of enumerating in advance all the ways of being unfree." With defeasible freedom, the title of protofreedom is truly deserved, for such a skeletal structure can only be developed further. It can only have the effect of providing for its own advancement and for that of the peoples who subscribe to it.

The conception of defeasible freedom sets up a very particular and worrisome future for those who would subscribe to it. Since defeasible freedom cannot progress without unfreedom, anyone who subscribes to it must, almost masochistically, invite impingement. That one's freedom is "defeasible" suggests, from any dictionary definition of defeasibility, that it is capable of being annulled. And Swanton's characterization of freedom will indeed be annulled, albeit not completely and not without benefit for coherence. As Swanton notes,

> [b]ecause freedom is a formal property, the principle of collocation of the freedom phenomena does not point to a single discriminable property that one or two otherwise identical objects can lack and the other possess. Rather the principle merely rationalizes the colloca-tion of a set of objects which have perhaps no material properties in common, and which cannot be exhaustively enumerated in advance. The reason "free" is defeasible is that unfree acts are those which in various ways breach certain standards, and the ways in which those breaches are manifested in specific stages of practical activity cannot be exhaustively specified in advance.[46]

To translate, the many and wise, thinking of their freedom, nevertheless cannot define or know it until it is threatened. Is it farfetched to say that Swanton's free persons do not exist until they are threatened? Certainly, one could live and act based upon one's endoxa alone, but such action could not clearly or coherently be an act of freedom. As a formal property, "freedom" is not substantive or cannot fully originate until it is breached or tested in practice against unfree acts.

That defeasible freedom progresses only when it is breached or threat-ened hints at the centrality of the effect of antifreedom for the origins of free peoples. But in contrast to the uncomplicated point that protofreedom and now antifreedom are both necessary effects produced for their origination, the point that Swanton draws from such "breaches" is that freedom then emerges as *useful* for free people. Thus,

> [t]he enriched Austinian picture of freedom developed in this chapter will enable us to satisfy the requirements of our background theory, for it will enable us to see the rationale of the extremely varied endoxa of freedom. The collocation of a heterogeneous range of phenomena as one and all *freedom* phenomena will be seen to have a distinctive point, viz., their perceived value as constitutive of one aspect of well-functioning human practical activity, viz., that which relates to *human potential in agency.*[47]

The point of all the endoxa collocated in the background theory will be their value to "*human potential in agency.*" In a nutshell the point of freedom is its usefulness, which was not discernible beforehand in the concept of defeasible freedom. As Swanton puts it, "[t]he perceived value of freedom lies in the value of realizing the various aspects of individual human potential in agency, for the actualization of potential in this area contributes to individual flourishing."[48]

With her point about "human flourishing," Swanton recalls the divergence first noted in my introduction to *The Origins of Free Peoples* between the usefulness accounts of their origins and an account that reiterates only their frenetic practices. Just as revolutionary explanations of origins emphasize the usefulness of freedom for free peoples against tyranny, so do philosophical explanations like that of Benn or Swanton emphasize that the main point of freedom is its usefulness for "agents." What both free citizens and philosophers of freedom forget, however, are their own ongoing efforts to produce protofreedom in the forms of natural persons or defeasible freedom. Protofreedom was not lying about like a ripe fruit ready to be harvested but a particular history produced for the sake of free peoples. Protofreedom is but an effect of this (frenetic) activity not a prior event.

Swanton: Anti-freedom

With "defeasible freedom," Swanton's protofreedom takes its full effect. Like Locke's state of nature or Benn's natural personality, Swanton's background theory is little more than the postulation that people are naturally free. It is also little more than a hint of something grander, which is exactly what is expected of a synecdoche. Swanton's plan to advance such protofreedom more fully therefore comes as no surprise to the student of origins. Thus:

> In Part II, I have endeavored to achieve coherence in the core area. In the next five chapters of part III, I shall examine, in turn, the relationships described in P1-P5 [5 propositions about the phenomena that make up unfreedom]. The aim is to determine the nature of those factors constituting unfreedom, thereby achieving coherence in the peripheral areas. The freedom phenomena will have been described in a way that saves the endoxa.[49]

By Part II of *Freedom*, coherence has been achieved where (in the "core area") it was not before; that is, the opinions of the wise and many were cohered as defeasible freedom. Part III deals with the other, "peripheral" area of *Freedom* and thereby also coheres "unfreedom" where that was not clear before. By comparing defeasible freedom against unfreedom, the "freedom phenomena" will be described in alignment with the initial intuitions and their point revealed.

Of course, exactly *how* such freedom becomes more coherent than before is a question of origins. Swanton claims that freedom, beginning as a mere collection of intuitions, emerges more coherently because of its usefulness to free people. But when Swanton's synecdoche is not forgotten, freedom is advanced not because of its usefulness so much as because of the efforts made on its behalf. And Swanton's plan reveals that the effort now required is indictment or the identification of antifreedom. This effort and its effect does not happen later in time or history. Just as Locke's free peoples were never historically first in some idyllic state of nature only to be threatened by injurers later, so too were Swanton's wise and many not first defeasibly free only to encounter threats or flaws of freedom later. Synecdoche and its effect of protofreedom and indictment and its effect of anti-freedom happen simultaneously and together constitute the origins of free peoples. (That they cannot be plainly presented simultaneously in this book is a defect of communication for which this author apologizes).

Unavailability of actions is charged as a type of "restraint" that contributes to the "unfreedom" of an agent. Such restraint "makes it impossible for an agent to do or avoid something." The relation between freedom and unavailability of actions here is crucial but not, Swanton insists, because we should be trying to assign moral responsibility to the one that restrains another. Swanton's objection to the assignation of moral responsibility as a way to determine "unavailability" does not prevent the indictment of

somebody who can be blamed. It simply means not to go about determining the restrainer as a moral threat but strictly as a threat to freedom.
The restrainer may indeed be a criminal and a violator of society's ethical
standards, but Swanton maintains that is another, separate determination.
For example, a wrongheaded determination of unavailability of actions
has included social conditions of inequality. Thus Swanton says that Benn
and Weinstein's argument, "Being Free to Act and Being a Free Man,"
mistakenly deals with whether or not the limitation of alternatives is
"just" or "unjust."[50] "Benn and Weinstein suggest, just social arrangements
are held to be part of the *normal* background conditions of choice." So
"presumably," Swanton counters quickly, this would mean that "just
imprisonment does not limit the freedom of prisoners."

Swanton's "deeper objection" is that Benn and Weinstein confuse the
difference between the values of justice and freedom. To consider just
background arrangements is to address the "*relationship* between individuals whose interests conflict but who nonetheless should be treated as
Kantian ends in themselves." However "the point of freedom is the value of
the absence of limitations inhibiting individual's potential." "We are better
off," Swanton advises, keeping these important value conceptions separate.
Of course, there can be a relation between unfreedom and justice as when
a good Samaritan is killed and so has his or her freedom terminated. But it
does not necessarily follow that only unjust actions limit freedom.

The point of Swanton's objections is to insist upon the pure determination
of this particular threat for the sake of freedom. Such a distinct determination is crucial if the usefulness of freedom is to be revealed against the
unavailability of actions. In Swanton's terms, "the point of freedom is the
value of the absence of limitations inhibiting individual's potential." This
important disclosure of freedom's point (not clear beforehand as mere
defeasible freedom) would not be possible if the unavailability of actions
were deemed antimoral or antijust. Readers should not be lulled into
inattention by the dry philosophical language here. It should be well noted
that the determination of this flaw of freedom is explicitly neither a just
nor a moral one. Presumably too, instigators of such "unfreedom" should
not in the first instance be considered unjust or immoral but strictly against
freedom. "On my view then, a restraint limits an agent's freedom, certeris
paribus, if it *restricts* the potential of that agent's practical activity, whether
justly or unjustly, legitimately or illegitimately."[51]

In the study of origins, however, the point of insisting on the pure determination of threat is not so that the meaning of freedom as useful to "agency"
may be made coherent but simply because the production of anti-freedom
or indictment must be accomplished precisely. Swanton says that a focus

upon the immorality or injustice of unavailability of actions detracts from "the point of freedom." That point is not its usefulness however, which is also a secondary matter, but the very effort that is the determination of anti-freedom or indictment. That is, what is evident first and foremost is the practice that determines unavailability of actions as a threat to freedom (and not to morality or justice). Such effort constitutes one special practice in the origins of free peoples that has been labeled here as indictment. Its effect is anti-freedom and the overall political point to be drawn is that without indictment and anti-freedom, freedom and those that subscribe to it could not advance or more fully originate. Swanton and her free peoples or agents might believe that the usefulness of their dearest value made the difference in how they arrived in their present, more coherent, circumstances. But it was simply their own efforts and practices all along.

With the charge of *ineligibility of actions*, Swanton again insists on determining only that threat and nothing else. That is, the indictment of this threat must be solely against freedom or anti-free. In this case the difficulty is that in the debate over ineligibility commentators too often argue that its determination is up to the agent confronting the restraint. The problem, says Swanton is that,

> they [current commentators in the literature] treat threats and offers as perlocutionary acts. A treatment of threats and offers as illocutionary acts would lead to quite different results. The reason . . . has to do with the conventions surrounding the making of offers and the context surrounding the proposal.[52]

So, it is the surrounding "context" that is key to knowing this flaw of freedom. Unlike unavailability of actions, ineligibility of actions depends upon knowing and including the idioms of language as well as social norms.

The practice of determining ineligibility is distinctive since it also includes the social context. Discerning this additional element is evident in the classic example of the highwayman. Typically if a robber, P, first puts a gun to Q's head and says "'I am going to kill you'" that is considered a threat. But if he later says, "'Your money or your life'" then this latter locution is an "offer," especially once Q gives up his money. Suppose further that Q were a "suicide" akratic who has been wanting to end his life but has thus far been unable to make the commitment. Is not the robber's proposal then an offer? Swanton insists however that it is a threat:

> Your money or your life' is text-book threatening language designed to invite the responses and sequels appropriate to threats; the context

is appropriate to the issuing of genuine threats—one of attempted armed robbery; the robber has the appropriate expectations and intentions: his aims are not those of the benevolent mercy killer, but are those of the traditional highway robber. In no way does the proposal have the illocutionary force of an offer.[53]

This passage definitely illustrates a threat that renders some actions ineligible. Swanton's development of its "context" was simply part of such indictment. The determination of "ineligibility" comes from its being an "illocutionary" act. And an illocutionary act is known as either threat or offer depending upon what is pronounced as the "context surrounding" it or the "conventions surrounding" it. Determining ineligibility is thus the particular charge that includes the "context" (e.g., such as the robber's "intentions" and that his proposal is "text-book" threatening language).

Swanton's grinding survey of "unfreedom" reveals that indictment comes in many forms and threats to freedom in innumerable shades. Their very variety and Swanton's dedication to the project of discerning them suggest that a similarly fascinated people would be instinctively coded to seek such threats. *Heteronomy*, for instance, consists of limitations on the "origins" of practical activity or agency. These "origins" (not to be confused with my account of origins) are "those mental states which can be broadly termed attitudes to action (whether pro, anti, or indifferent)." So heteronomy is a flaw in "practical activity *qua* practical activity." Specifically, according to Swanton,

> limitations denoted by "heteronomy" occur in the processes of acquiring desires and beliefs, linking these in deliberation (where this occurs), and forming practical judgements and intentions (whether or not these are the termination of a process of deliberation).[54]

From this initial and broad determination of the flaw, Swanton goes on to note that heteronomy can be of two kinds. First, heteronomy can consist in those limitations which render practical activity "irrational." Second, heteronomy may be the limitation that renders practical action "inauthentic." Both limitations, irrationality and inauthenticity, can be found in those "states" that give rise to practical action.

Interestingly, Swanton admits to having little facts to go on to precisely determine the heteronomy of *irrationality*. She recognizes the difficulties involved in specifying rationality, much less irrationality. Nonetheless the determination of both terms is not impossible. Thus:

> What should be the standards of rationality for human beings in their diverse activities and roles is a vast and difficult topic outside the scope of this book. One further point related to freedom must however be reemphasized. I have said that standards of rationality appropriate to human freedom are those appropriate to the flourishing of humans in their various stages of development and "'denouement.'" Standards of rationality appropriate to the freedom of infants, children and the senile are those appropriate to those phases of human development and demise![55]

With this to-each-his-own notion of rationality in hand, Swanton goes on to attack the association between "models of rationality" and freedom. Swanton does not subscribe to those "autonomy" views where, for example, children are said not to meet some standard of mastering high rationality. On the one hand, if conditions of autonomy admit of "degree" than the moral precept of equal respect for persons is neglected because some will be more deserving of freedom than others. But if autonomy is said to have a rationality "threshold" then that must be specified. On both counts, the "task is impossible of fulfillment, however."[56]

But while Swanton is unable to determine irrationality by reference to models of rationality, she is able to do so by reference to different categories of persons and their accompanying rationalities. Swanton set the groundwork for this determination with her idea of denouement or "phases of freedom." If it is difficult to distinguish between degrees of rationality, one can distinguish between infants, children, adults, and the senile. Swanton therefore accedes to,

> the view that autonomy is a developmental concept admitting of degree. I shall also concede that the fact that autonomy as a degree concept would license differing treatments of individuals in respect of their freedom. The moral requirement of according equal respect to all autonomous agents, however, does not entail a requirement of equal treatment in respect of freedom ... According equal respect may actually require unequal treatment in proportion to differing merits, degrees of competence, and degrees of potentiality and capacity.[57]

So every type of individual has freedom tailored for them. One perhaps political implication of this logic is a defense of unequal treatment.

For instance, Swanton notes that, "[i]t is indeed true that 'the sliding scale conception of autonomy' may 'allow differing degrees of paternalistic intervention.'" Yet "such differences would not necessarily violate the principle of equal respect." Swanton abruptly completes her section on irrationality with this unanswered question:

> We should treat children and adults with "equal respect" because they have equal worth in Gregory Vlastos's sense, but does this imply that, if adults should not be subjected to compulsory education, children should not be as well?[58]

Since Swanton immediately moves on to discuss the other heteronomy form of "inauthenticity," she must consider the answer to her question to be self-evident, perhaps intuitively so. Based upon her discussion of rationality in terms of "denouement" the answer to her question is no, "adults" are free in such a way that they should not be compulsorily educated as are most "children." In terms of Swanton's "phases of freedom," adults are at a stage where they cannot be compelled to be educated while children can be so compelled.

As Swanton's only example in this heteronomy section is the compulsory education example, the flaw of irrationality must be discernible whenever the "adult" does *not* meet the degree of rationality that otherwise frees her from being so compelled. If the relation between rationality and freedom depends upon one's phase of freedom, then irrationality must be when the "adult" is out of phase. According to Swanton the criteria for such determinations are always particular and complex. It "depends on the context and nature of the differing treatments and on the reasons for those differences."[59] The compulsory education example that contrasts the treatment of adults compared with children makes this point obvious. Adults have adult rationality and children do not. Analogously, rational adults have it while irrational adults do not. But the interesting problem that arises from this account of irrationality is that for those between the ages of approximately 12 and 112, or between childhood and senility, there remains no established consensus on the meaning of their rationality.

The only way to break this stalemate yet determine irrationality anyway is simply to allege irrationality and to maintain it by repeating that indictment furiously: Whoever is not an adult when they should be is irrational. Since rationality was admittedly too difficult to define, irrationality originates simply through the charge of impropriety, of being other than what one should be, or of being out of proper "phase." The practice of indicting irrationality is what makes the threatening effect of irrationality available. Indeed, this interesting determination depends upon pure indictment since irrationality was discernible despite the admitted lack of criteria of rationality for those ranging in age from 12 to 112. Irrationality thus does not reveal, as Swanton would like, that freedom is useful to agents and their "flourishing." It reveals only that it is an entirely produced effect replicated in Swanton's intensive account of origins.

The same pure technique of charging antifreedom is found again when the other form of heteronomy known as *inauthenticity* is addressed. Swanton's advice is to determine this flaw *in situ* and therefore by contrast with what would be an improvement at that moment. What is to be avoided in considering inauthenticity is to begin with a definition of autonomy or some key feature thereof and then identify its violation since *a priori* definitions do not always provide the best guides for agency. They could lead people away from coherent freedom (i.e., away from flourishing in their agency). Instead, the determination of inauthenticity is its threat to agency in context, that is, in contrast with what would be more useful action at that moment. The charge of inauthenticity is the declaration, "that is a threat to freedom because another action then would enhance agency." In sum, the threat or flaw of inauthenticity is one who should then do otherwise.

For example, "context" supplies the means by which Swanton determines the particular inauthenticity known as "nonidentification." Swanton emphasizes context because, given the dynamism of practical activity, the various possibilities of inauthenticity cannot all be anticipated by any one theorist nor contained in any single definition. Swanton therefore corrects the autonomy writers, this time for trying to define "nonidentification" based upon features of autonomy. Their,

> error is the failure to recognize that factors such as nonidentification, nonintegration, etc., are material properties of autonomy that constitute limitations on flourishing in agency only in certain contexts. For the anorexic who experiences the healthy appetite as opposed to the obsessive desire for slimness as a fetter, "liberation"' is obtained not by eliminating the desire with which she does not identify, but by eliminating the nontemperate second-order desire for slimness. Nonidentification here is a sign of hope for recovery to healthy agency rather than constitutive of heteronomy. Similarly the failure of the demeaned woman to integrate her desires to be a "good housewife" with her lower-order desires to escape her situation—desires marked

by "urges and longings"—is not in that context a limitation. Rather, in that kind of context, it would be integration that is the limitation.[60]

Just because one possesses tidy definitions of autonomy features such as identification or integration does not necessarily mean that they help determine limitations upon such autonomy. Indeed, it can turn out to be just the opposite. Swanton shows that the "demeaned woman" would simply continue in that condition if her desires were united as according to the dictate of autonomy as integration. She would be better off, freedom-wise, disintegrating a bit and then honing in on her desire to escape circumstances. Until then, in this case as well as in that of the anorexic, integration and identification are inauthenticities. The lesson is that relying upon definitions of autonomy to discern inauthenticity is not an assured way to determine that limitation and so some other kind of procedure is needed.

For Swanton, the payoff from addressing inauthenticity is that it draws forth the usefulness of freedom, but for the student of origins it reveals a most capricious and capacious form of indictment. The threat of inauthenticity in a free society turns out to be ever present since some at least marginally better outcome is always possible with any and every action. The Monday-morning quarterback can always point out that another play would have been superior. To include "what might have been" as a form of antifreedom or "flaw of freedom" is to entrap subscribers in a worrisome net no matter what they do. Swanton's point that inauthenticity draws out how agency can flourish pales against the possibility that such a gross charge could be leveled at any moment. Since an inauthentic threat is "one who should then do otherwise," the context for such a breezy charge could always be constructed. That the anorexic is better off eating than not and the demeaned woman is better off escaping than not are powerful examples. But what is to prevent the same charge of inauthenticity from being applied to anyone that is not meeting their supposed potential such as loiterers on a sidewalk who should 'move along' or the homeless who ought to enter a shelter for the night? The test of inauthenticity provides insight not into the usefulness of liberty so much as insight into the extent to which antifreedom can be located at any time, anywhere, and so illustrates to what degree indictment is part and parcel of the origins of free peoples.

Conclusion

At last, free people originate, "coherently" or simply more fully than before. Swanton's major revelation is that freedom involves the "significance of actions" or "interests" (i.e., its usefulness for free people or "agents.") The interests of an agent can be ascribed precisely when the limits upon his or her actions (i.e., the various "flaws" of freedom) are determined and so the value of freedom to his or her interests and flourishing becomes apparent. While not coherent beforehand, as mere defeasible freedom, the usefulness of one's freedom becomes clear each time it is tested against distinct threats ranging from unavailability of actions to inauthenticity. If free peoples do not at first know the full value or meaning of their liberty, they do so after such a lengthy test. In the philosophical sense, free people originate more coherently with the recognition of the usefulness of their agency.

But a notable chink in the armor of the usefulness thesis appears when Swanton admits that even the "addict" who continues the habit has found such freedom to be in his interests. It is a claim that questions the traditional relation between freedom and usefulness. Thus:

> Wall discusses the case of the heroin addict who would prefer the life of addiction to alternatives. It is possible that, under hypothetical conditions such as those being described, a person would not express a preference for a life governed by a want to live a "worthwhile"' life of achievement, say. Let us suppose that this person would not care to live a long life, that he would do anything to avoid pain, frustration, anxiety. Finally, let us suppose that his character is such that he finds the stresses of modern life intolerable and that there is no real prospect of being able to change his character. On my account of interests, it is possible for it to be in that person's interests to remain an addict.[61]

Perhaps not a few of Swanton's readers might hope that she would deny the usefulness thesis in this extreme case. Not without cause, the nonphilosopher might think that a life of addiction is hardly free. Swanton indicates acquaintance with the criticism of her argument as a short-sighted, want-regarding, or "'subjectivist'" account of interests; the addict's interests should instead "lie in his 'good' or 'advantage' understood objectively." Indeed addiction, in the sense of dependency upon drug usage, would seem to be the opposite of what it means to be free. Yet Swanton maintains her position. Why?

Swanton's defense of the addict does not merely expose the difficulty of upholding the usefulness thesis for the origins of free peoples in every case but recalls the other thesis of origins rooted in liberation. The reason that

Swanton can defend the agency of the addict is because freedom ultimately relies upon frenetic practices not its usefulness. In Swanton's terms:

> The experience test allows the agent herself, under idealized conditions, to determine just what sacrifices and costs are to be borne in the pursuit of an ideal life in the various complex and deficient circumstances in which she finds herself.[62]

Whereas the nonphilosopher and Wall demand a virtuous standard of freedom for the addict, otherwise it is not a free life, Swanton's test states that the coherence of freedom varies with the agent's experience as, for example, the totality of "circumstances" in the life of the addict. That experience includes the production of protofreedom or a hazy presupposition of agency and the production of anti-freedom or what Swanton calls here the "deficient circumstances in which she finds herself." Admittedly, Swanton's terminology is different, but the origins of free peoples remain the same. Swanton's defense of the free addict draws out how necessary it is to produce proto-freedom and anti-freedom. Usefulness and interests have no part in the matter of the growth, progress, or advancement of free people; those ascriptions are afterthoughts.

The point of this example is that Swanton comes close to admitting that the origins of free peoples, addicts or no, depend upon the productive practices of synecdoche and indictment or, in a word, liberation. Defeasible freedom is a form of proto-freedom that handily sets the stage for the advancement of free people or "agents." And "deficient circumstances" is another name for anti-freedom or the threat that spurs such advancement. With her insistence upon usefulness or what she calls "interests" Swanton does not take the final, perhaps fateful, step that would recall the origins of free peoples solely in terms of liberation. Of the two explanations, usefulness or liberation, William of Ockham would be pleased with the latter, more parsimonious, and direct thesis. But it is today not the most intuitive and unfortunately intuitions have become the ruinous starting point in too much of the political philosophy of freedom.

In *Twilight of the Idols* Nietzsche argued that one of the fallacies of post-Platonic thinking is a tendency to mistake the effect for the cause.[63] In this case, an effect, the usefulness of freedom for those who subscribe to it, has been mistaken as the cause or reason for its advancement. Both Benn and Swanton like freedom and so do free peoples. In Swanton's more technical terms they find it in their interests. So then, as Nietzsche would say, they "cast about in the blue" for ways to argue that dear freedom originates because of its usefulness. But again, as Nietzsche warned, "[h]owever well one has understood the utility of any physiological organ (or of a legal institution, a social custom, a political usage, a form in art or in a religious cult), this means nothing regarding its origin."[64]

The origins of free peoples and their favorite value have nothing to do with whether freedom is useful, in their interests, or well liked and worth a fight. None of the components found in the usefulness account of origins, such as Swanton's defeasible freedom or the threat of inauthenticity, are possible without the practices that enable them. Both the freedom deemed so useful and those distinct peoples that adopt it as their paramount value are *effects* of particular, ongoing, frenetic practices or origins. In a nutshell, it is liberation that is the motor behind these examples, not useful, beloved liberty. Some proto-freedom, be it the natural personality or defeasible freedom, is projected as the hazy version of the liberty to come. And some anti-freedom, perhaps psychopathy or inauthenticity, is postulated as a threat to freedom. They are all effects of identifiable, replicable practices.

The careful philosophical expositions of Benn and Swanton imply a political society of a wistful and a wary people. Their synecdoches translate onto the scale of such society into extraordinary effort devoted to producing and simulating the distinct history of a people as initially and primarily free. The frequent proclamations of the self-evidence or naturalness of human freedom, fireworks displays marking dates of full independence, history textbooks referring to a prior era of near-blissful self-government, and exhortations and advertisements to exercise one's choice in various venues all reproduce proto-freedom. Meanwhile politicians' railings, media emphases, and the impacts of the military and prison industrial complexes perpetuate the idea of being surrounded by threats to freedom.[65] As these threats are not characterized as threats to their equality, their justice, or to any feature or value besides their liberty, they earn the distinct label of anti-freedom that can be traced back to the practice of indictment.

What matters the difference between the rational usefulness thesis versus the frenetic liberation thesis? The difference between a people wedded to liberty because of its usefulness rather than because of their own frenetic efforts is the difference between a politics that in its encounters with others will "force them to be free" versus a politics capable of genuinely attempting other entreaties. It is the difference between a politics that lashes out against inhabitants of a presumed imperfect, even hostile, world and a politics that regretfully sacrifices honorable enemies. In the next chapter, I present evidence of the ongoing and tremendous effort of obscuration that has so far prevented these other, less damaging, political alternatives and instead holds the free peoples hostage to a misread fortune.

Notes

1. Attributed to Michel Foucault by Ivison, *Political Argument*, vi.
2. See Bauman, *Freedom* or Donohue, *Freedom from Want*. The intellectual times have certainly changed. Marcuse identified comsumerism as a form of voluntary servitude; Marcuse, *Essay on Liberation*, 11.
3. "The point of repetition is to change not just people's minds but also their very brains. If they had succeeded in getting their view of freedom into the brains of all, or even most, Americans then they could take freedom as they define it for granted," Lakoff, *Whose Freedom*, 9.
4. Nietzsche, *Twilight*, 103.
5. De Beauvoir, *Ambiguity*, 32.
6. Resnick, "Locke," 102. Gough cites historians who claim that legal history simply did not interest Locke, while Gough himself speculates that it was irrelevant for Locke's purposes. See Gough, "James Tyrrell," 587–8.
7. Caro, "Onlookers," 920.
8. Fukuyama, *End of History*.
9. Ashcraft, *Revolutionary Politics*.
10. Huntington, *Who are We?*
11. Benn, *A Theory*, 215.
12. Ibid., 32.
13. Ibid., 28.
14. Ibid., 61.
15. Ibid., 63.
16. Ibid., 63.
17. Ibid., 77.
18. Ibid., 62.
19. Ibid., 90–91.
20. Ibid., 122.
21. Ibid., 92.
22. Ibid., 118–19.
23. Ibid., 126.
24. Ibid., 157.
25. Ibid., 155.
26. Ibid., 100–101.
27. Ibid., 156–57.
28. Ibid., 159.
29. Ibid., 160.
30. Ibid.
31. One of the problems with this characterization of psychopathy is that it matches many prevailing notions that esteem "instant gratification." Benn must

therefore spend some time trying to make the distinction between psychopathy and what many free citizens today seem to be doing.

32. Ibid., 161.

33. Ibid., 163.

34. Ibid., 163–64.

35. On "fascination" see Baudrillard, "Ideological," 255.

36. Swanton, *Freedom*, 15.

37. "My view differs from Rawls's in that conceptions are not compared with the theorist's initial convictions, but with the endoxa." Swanton, *Freedom*, 61.

38. Ibid., 193–94.

39. Ibid., 24.

40. Ibid., 30.

41. Ibid., 29.

42. Ibid., 38.

43. Ibid., 33.

44. Ibid., 33.

45. "If liberty is simply to be let alone . . . liberty appears as stunted, sterile, thing . . ." McCloskey, "A Critique," 486–87. Schneider refers to such freedom as "void or vacuum." Schneider, "The Liberties," 657.

46. Swanton, *Freedom*, 48.

47. Ibid., 49. "We need to propose a hypothesis about the distinctive point of classifying a range of phenomena as freedom phenomena . . . This point is given by the value that freedom is perceived to possess . . . The hypothesis is: (T1) The perceived value of freedom lies in the value of realizing the various aspects of individual human potential in agency, for the actualization of potential in this area contributes to individual flourishing." Ibid., 46–47.

48. Ibid., 38–39.

49. Ibid., 88.

50. Ibid., 99.

51. Ibid., 100.

52. Ibid., 106.

53. Ibid., 108–9.

54. Ibid., 118.

55. Ibid., 122.

56. Ibid., 122.

57. Ibid., 123.

58. Ibid., 123.

59. Ibid., 123.

60. Ibid., 134–35.

61. Ibid., 174–75.

62. Ibid., 175.

63. Nietzsche, *Twilight*, 59.

64. Nietzsche, *Basic Writings*, 513.

65. Dillon, *Politics*, 15.

5

Secrets of Freedom

The study of the origins of free peoples terminates in a barbed thought. Free peoples are enabled by the unawareness of their origins. The old saying that ignorance is bliss is essentially prepolitical when it implies a passive predisposition, but the idea becomes politically interesting when unawareness is both sought after and imperative for the final product.[1] The origins of the free peoples, as the practices that enable them today, yesterday, and tomorrow, depend upon the production of special ambiguities, of secrets. The pattern of producing such ambiguity is most prominently found in famous chronicles such as Locke's *Second Treatise* or Jefferson's *Declaration*. For instance, it is still not uncommon, although it remains charming, to hear that free persons were simply born that way or that they are self-evidently or naturally free. For perhaps three centuries, if not longer, such assertions have proven to be a sufficient basis for the establishment and the maintenance of a free society. Along a similar vein, many philosophers today need state only that freedom begins as a hazy intuition or as a collocation of intuitions. From then on, the objective is to simply clarify what is already in place, no matter the ambiguity of its beginnings.

Of course, it might be asked, how could it be otherwise for the origins of the free peoples are so distant in the past that they must now be obscure? But not every sort of free people has had such indefinite beginnings. What Constant distinguished as the "liberty of the ancients" rose and fell with the fortunes of their beloved republics.[2] But the origins of the modern free peoples are supposedly not bound by place or time. They are always born as free as indeed they believe all peoples are if only they or their current governors would acknowledge that "fact" of nature. Free peoples today would also not, for example, claim that their freedom originates as a franchise or charter from their king or other earthly lord. Yet that quite traceable source was essentially the mode of freedom's origins during the High Middle Ages.[3] Therefore, the indefinite beginnings of elements crucial for their freedom has not been an automatic feature of free peoples.

Given their own insistence on indefinite origins, the possibility must at last be considered that the contemporary free peoples need their origins to be imperfectly understood. After all, whether the first instantiation of their liberty was a self-evident truth, a mythical state of nature, or a set of intuitions or ordinary language locutions, such indefinite beginnings have not hindered the free peoples. Indeed, the sheer weight of historical evidence indicates that they have been quite successful with just such imperfectly formulated origins not only at the international, political, and societal levels but in their artistic and philosophical expressions as well. In this book, as an inquiry into origins, the writings of contemporary philosophers such as Benn and Swanton have earned extra scrutiny for this question precisely because of their sustained and explicit efforts to achieve clarity of expression. Hence their formulations of freedom's origins as indefinite or "intuitive" cannot be read as rhetoric nor as best guesses for an impossible historical question. Instead, their thoughtful underformulations of freedom's first instantiation as intuitions or as natural states, imperfect as they are conceptually, are clues of great importance. Such repeated underformulations are not theoretical half-measures as these same hazy expressions can be found in writings on high liberty for over three centuries. They are also not mistakes because if they ever had interrupted the life of the free peoples they would have stopped using them long ago.

But such imperfect recollection is only one part of the story for not only are the origins of their liberty indefinite, so too are the origins of those who threaten the free. The importance of such threats stems from how they served as the spur for those celebrated revolutions, such as the Glorious, American, or French Revolutions, that advanced, secured, and instituted the latent liberty of the free peoples. To be sure, those who threaten free peoples today are identified readily enough, say, as tyrants, criminals, or terrorists, but exactly why these fearsome beings "hate our freedoms" or how they originated as such remains unclear. For Locke, those who threaten liberty are described as injurers and are to be treated as one would a rabid "lion" or a "wolf." Similarly Jefferson, in his famous *Declaration of Independence*, identified King George III as posing a threat in a variety of ways to the liberty of an American people. Yet the origins of these particular threats, as threats specifically against liberty, remain obscure even though precisely those threats are pivotal enough that they further the arguments of Locke and Jefferson as the rationale for the more full political advancement of their free peoples.

It might seem eminently reasonable to claim that threats to the free are such a pressing problem that the question of their origins is a frivolous diversion. But even if free peoples have required quick action in the face of such threats, which has included violent revolution or defensive wars, would not further clarity on the question of their origins dramatically aid in that defense? For instance, given such tactical insight, could not the forces of freedom then more carefully target the weaknesses of their foes? Yet even contemporary philosophers of liberty, who today stand as the beneficiaries of centuries of hindsight and experience, are not clear on the matter of the origins of threats to free peoples. Thinkers such as Benn and Swanton are quite able to describe such threats in more subtle shades and hues than either Locke or Jefferson identified in their famous chronicles of origins. As has been noted, there can be threats to the "coherence of freedom" such as "executive failure" and "heteronomy" or threats to the psychic health of the "free personality" in the forms of "psychosis" and "schizophrenia." But the question of the origins of these injurious conditions, not in descriptive medical, symptomatic, or psychological terms, but specifically as threats to freedom is consistently underemphasized. Instead, what is typically said to matter and what these careful thinkers suggest should be on our collective radar screen is simply that our precious freedom is in peril. It then follows that the coherence or the clarity of freedom must be secured against that which detracts from it just as, on the physical scale of politics, the security of a free society must be protected against those who threaten it. In either case, philosophical or political, the question of the origins of the threats to free peoples can remain indefinite since, in the face of such peril, an immediate defensive response to the problem is seen as the pragmatic priority.

The point is that the imperfect knowledge of origins has been perfect for that type of free people whose origins are indefinite and whose threats also have indefinite origins. Free peoples have been successful precisely without a clear knowledge of the origins of the various threats that they have faced just as they have managed quite well precisely without a clear knowledge of the origins of their own liberty. Locke's Englishmen and Jefferson's Americans have, according to some accounts, done well enough that their freedom has been worth championing for other, as yet unfree, peoples too.[4] It is therefore finally time to recognize that the imperfect understanding of their freedom's origins, including the indefinite origins of the threats to their freedom, does not detract from but rather enables the free peoples. That is, not only do the free peoples misunderstand the origins of those who threaten their liberty, but they also should not understand them. If so, there is a curious irony that such peoples, born of Europe's age of the Enlightenment with its ideal of the dissemination of knowledge, must not know themselves too well.

The aim of this chapter is to summarize how the free peoples actively work to obscure or to not clearly understand the origins of their freedom and their threats. Such obscuration or construction of ambiguity is a central feature in the experience of the free peoples and their peculiar mode of liberty. For example, the determination of threats found in innumerable political speeches, in philosophical writings, and even in courts of law do not progress much beyond repeated public identification and pointing fingers. In any of these forums, whether the political, philosophical, or the juridical, the particular practices involved in determining threats to free persons simply cannot produce a clear knowledge of their origins. To be sure, a knowledge of the name of a cognitive threat to liberty such as akrasia, or a knowledge of the location of a criminal, can be developed but the other knowledge of their origins is consistently neglected. When this trail of ambiguity is followed rigorously, it turns out that the free peoples have not and cannot really care about the origins of criminality, tyranny, terrorism, or other such threats, for that would mean to care for something other than their paramount value, which is "obviously" in peril. The practical focus, then, centers upon the fact that the threat is "out there." After all, has it not been identified, named, and described by the courts, philosophers, politicians, or journalists reporting on the evening news? The location of the danger is clear and present. What do origins matter when dear liberty needs to be secured immediately against that obvious threat?

The origins of free peoples matter if they are imperative or "necessary."[5] If a free people are possible only with indefinite origins then the practices that produce such particular effects matter a very great deal. Furthermore, if such origins matter that much then it would not be unexpected that the free peoples might actively work in their politics, in their educational systems, in their philosophy, in their jurisprudence, in their media, and in their everyday lives to ensure that their origins remain secret. Such necessary and ongoing work of obscuration might be called, in a nutshell, the reproduction of secret origins. The crucial ambiguities found in chronicles of origins are persistent and prevalent, so much so that it must be considered that such indefinitely understood origins enable the familiar and happy effect known as a free people. The format of expression makes little difference to this pattern of origination since historical accounts, political speeches, poetic narratives, newspaper editorials, media reports, and careful treatises of political philosophy alike are all uniformly unclear on the origins of the free peoples. Such a pattern should come as no surprise since their freedom, as a particular effect requiring particular origins, requires its own imperative practices and effects no matter whether it is developed in thought, in writing, or on the grand scale of a society.

The origins of free peoples have been indefinite for a long time and this is the case no matter whether one consults the early modern thought of Sidney or Locke, Jefferson's enlightened pronouncement of the independence of an American people, or intensive, post-Rawlsian, writings on liberty from Benn and Swanton. It has gone on for so long, in fact, that it is high time to admit that there is a particular tradition of free peoples that require that their origins remain indefinite. In contrast to the classic Lipset thesis, which suggested that a certain high standard of living and education is needed for a free society to flourish, the student of origins claims that a special sort of unawareness is imperative. The persistence of particular ambiguities in chronicles of the origins of free peoples (or their gross preponderance in their collective memory) is the evidentiary proof of its political advantage. In the tradition of their freedom, whether in their philosophical, historical, political, or artistic expressions, the systematic underformulation of the origins of free peoples is central to the possibility of their particular mode of life. To put this analysis another way, the contemporary free peoples need their forgetful origins. But the process of forgetting, as Nietzsche taught, is not a passive but an active, energetic process.[6] Like the legend of nurturing Memnosyne, who protected her children by providing them with false memories, the active forgetting of information is achieved not merely when selected memories are withheld but also when others are implanted. The program of enabling the free peoples, their origination so to speak, is conducted at no less a scale than the whole of free society and it entails massive, ongoing, and proactive efforts to underformulate the origins of their freedom. Included in this program is the parallel underdetermination of the origins of those who threaten the free.

Perfect Origins

The demonstration of the origins of free peoples depends, like a math proof, upon the replicability of its practices and effects. So rather than casually attributing their initial spark of freedom to intuitions, self-evident truths, nature, essence, or some other hazy history and then hurriedly advancing to defend such freedom when threatened, the student of origins reiterates precisely such hazy formulations of freedom's first instance as a produced or posited effect. The effect is of such import as to be worthy of its own name: *protofreedom.* This term exactly highlights the enabling effect of a state of nature or those proverbial "intuitions" of liberty when put forth as the first instantiation of the freedom to come in a chronology of a free people. With protofreedom in place, whether in philosophic writing or in the mind of a free citizenry, it is then possible for liberty to be threatened and advanced. In order to emphasize the exact originary practice involved for this pivotal effect, the student of origins goes on to replicate the practice that posits such protofreedom. This particular practice is called *synecdoche,*which is a term from the field of rhetoric for a practice that posits only a portion of a larger concept but a portion that can easily be associated with that larger concept. A synecdoche sets the stage for the further development of a desired outcome whether philosophically or in the future of a people's history (and so, in the temporal dimension, this synecdoche is also an *anabasis,* another rhetorical term meaning to postulate so as to set the stage for the future). To put all of this succinctly, free peoples make a biased history for themselves. Indeed, there cannot even be a question of whether it is biased or not, for they must have that fraction, hint, inkling, or smidgeon of their sort of freedom set in their past if they are to ever advance their freedom more fully through revolution or reform.

The replication of the origins of free peoples also includes the production, construction, or the refinement of those who threaten them, or threats to freedom. Such threats are a specific type since, after all, they are not said to threaten a racial, class, religious or occupational group but only the free. But they are also even more specific than that because their origins are also invariably indefinite. For example, it is typically not known why Locke's injurer or Jefferson's tyrant decided to threaten liberty. Usually, it is said that injurers are not using right reason (an explanation which begs the questions of their particular origins; why this individual but not that one?) or that such threats are simply to be expected in an imperfect human world (which is a presumption that halts further inquiry into the question of their origins). But instead of nonchalantly ascribing the source of those who threaten free peoples to an imperfect world or worse, to an imperfect humanity, the student of origins duplicates the exact procedure that posits and refines threats to the free. In this regard the term *antifreedom* has been deployed, following the examples of Nancy or Brown because it is perhaps the only term that can indicate an effect that is both against free peoples and a part of their origins. A name for the practice that produces so pivotal an effect is *indictment,* which means here to charge, indict, or simply to point out a threat to freedom.

These interjections at moments of indefiniteness in the chronicles of free peoples (e.g., protofreedom, antifreedom, synecdoche, indictment) result in a fully practical rendition of origins that augments the familiar accounts precisely at the points where they refuse to inform. Admittedly in what has been called the liberal tradition of political writing, the authors are also insistent upon the practicality or pragmatism of their views of liberty (or for liberty as "practical activity" in Swanton's parlance).[7] Certainly, based on these often impassioned writings, who wouldn't defend dear liberty in the face of unattractive constraints such as Locke's "state of war" or Jefferson's infuriating King George? Mounting such a defense will strike many observers almost instinctively as the practical course of action. But when it comes to identifying the origins of the actors involved, these same practical thinkers are less forthcoming in their writings and ascribe the emergence of the free and their threats, both absolutely crucial elements in their chronicles, to everything from hazy intuitions or divine will to sheer "contingency" and "human weakness." By contrast, *The Origins of Free Peoples* augments such forgetful political thinking with the practices that have been used for their chronicle and thereby enable their freedom once more.

After only a bit of observation, particular patterns of activity become noticeable in the origins of free peoples. For example, not only is the indefiniteness of the origins of both their freedom and their threats commonplace but it must also be just the right measure of indefiniteness. For example, the typical starting point in the chronicle or the philosophy of a free people is formulated with seemingly unproblematic postulations such as intuitions, self-evident truths, states of nature, the cheery assertion that they were born as free and the like. But every such conceptualization of protofreedom, while ambiguous or indefinite, is also always carefully modulated to a precise *valence*. Were it too well conceptualized or too unambiguous there would not be a need for protofreedom to be advanced in political thinking or in political life. Locke's state of nature, Jefferson's self-evident truth of Americans' initially free condition, or the notion that humans are simply born free are all examples of how initially underdeveloped formulations set the stage for more liberty to come. But on the other hand, if protofreedom were too faint or underformulated, there would not be enough freedom to come under threat. There would then not be enough freedom to fret about, or alternatively, a people would not then be free enough to worry about threats to their freedom and the celebrated revolutions that advanced their cause would never have happened. Proto-freedom, therefore, always requires a careful, *perfect modulation*. It is no coincidence that so many commentators and politicians, as well as contemporary philosophers of liberty, manage to live so easily with ambivalent formulations of its origins and even propose it themselves. It is because free birth, divine endowments, states of nature, intuitions, background theories, or the naturally free personality are not inadequate or second-best formulations. They are also not the best guesses that mere mortals can make about the emergence of freedom's opening instance or about the basic character of free humanity. But they are the perfect postulations for a familiar, ongoing mode of liberty. Diderot once declared that "freedom is a gift from heaven."[8] But while Diderot's heaven might be generous to a people for one day or perhaps two, the exact valences required for the free peoples are unlikely to be granted continuously for centuries. For precisely such ambiguity to be maintained requires quite human politics, institutions, and decisions that accept some policies and reject others on an ongoing basis according to the exact tolerances of indefiniteness that are required. A one-time gift or endowment is simply not enough for a free people to successfully persist.

What is morally worrisome about the origins of free peoples, as the precise modulation of imperative effects, is that those who are said to threaten the free are then also produced effects. They do not simply arise from "God knows where." And they are not simply hostile to the free peoples, period and end of the story. Frankly, observers should be skeptical of the politicians' explanations of plain hostility to free societies because they are prone to be self-aggrandizing or jingoistic. They imply that free peoples are threatened simply because they are free and their enemies cannot stand that happy condition. However the origins of such threats, in terms of what is required for antifreedom, simply cannot be that hazy. This is because the familiar chronology of freedom, threat, and advancement relies upon a formulation of threat that must be carefully calibrated.

Anti-freedom is a precisely modulated effect because if the threat it presents were too strong, if such wickedness were too powerful, then defending freedom against it would not be the pragmatic response so much as some other counterstrategy such as stoic acceptance or even collaboration. On the other hand, if the threat of anti-freedom were only an irritation, the celebrated, revolutionary defenses of freedom would not be a practical response because then, assuming that Locke's chronicle provides a model, a proto-free people could remain more or less content in their proto-free states of nature. Even the philosophers of liberty, with their quite careful descriptions of threats to liberty ranging from imperfection and "deficiency" to "flaws," must postulate the exact valence that is needed for anti-freedom: threatening but not overly so.

In general, the source of threats to free peoples is often pronounced as a function of the "imperfection" of human nature or "human weakness."[9] Such hurtful and misanthropic pronouncements are certainly familiar enough. The implication of claims that the world or humanity is imperfect basically means that while its threats are unwelcome they are also unexceptional. They exist and are of concern, but to even ask of their origins is practically ridiculous for they are of the world, which is imperfect or flawed. Whether or not this is an accurate characterization of the moral world, universe, or human condition is one question. But whether or not such imperfection enables the possibility and life of free peoples is another question and it has a clear answer.

The precise valence of threat means that those who menace free peoples, the anti-free, require too much specialized refinement or what Foucault called "discipline" to originate because of the natural imperfection of humanity or the world. The whole world would have to be politically oriented toward the needs of the free. It would have to be so mechanical, not to mention perversely generous, as to supply the free peoples with perfectly modulated threats every time, for decades, even centuries. Such threats could not, for instance, be threats to clan, ethnic, or religious integrity, or to party dignity.[10] They could only be threats to the free that, over a length of time and given their distinctive modulation, can only be a repeatedly produced, refined, and perfected effect. Unfortunately, the deduction is not made that an imperfect world or humanity would be either too chaotic or too indifferent to steadily provide threats at the proper tolerances that have been needed throughout the long and successful history of the free peoples. It is also never considered, or perhaps it is too difficult to contemplate, that only their own, forgotten, and quite productive efforts have sustained them.

Definitions

The overall picture that emerges from the study of the origins of free peoples is that such beings live in their own world. They have their own unique political ecology or habitus. The reason that free life is a closed political world of their own making is because nothing is gained or lost in the origination process and what those efforts produce. The practices of synecdoche and indictment enable free peoples perfectly, as they must, since their particular style of liberty would be impossible otherwise. With their origins now fully recalled, the totality of these practices and effects turns out to be what Zizek dubs a "loop," cycle, recurrence, or as Schelling put it, "a system" that alternately detracts from and provides for itself.[11] On the one hand, protofreedom is produced, thereby setting the political and the philosophical stage for the further advancement of itself. On the other hand, anti-freedom is identified thereby providing the rationale for why there should be reform, revolution, or even just wars to more fully secure and advance protofreedom.[12] By postulating proto-freedom, Locke, Jefferson, and other chroniclers set the stage for a politics in which there is a particular kind of free people that can be threatened and so revolutionary or other strong reform must be undertaken to further "secure" their liberty. And indeed how could such scrawny initial liberty as proto-freedom not become threatened in any real human world? "For no age has been as insecure and mortally endangered as this our own insistently secured one."[13]

To rewrite the celebrated chronicles of free peoples in the terminology of origins is to say that a synecdoche produces the history that there was already some fraction of freedom in place to be threatened. In addition, by identifying a threat like Locke's "lyon" or Jefferson's King George as a threat not to party, ethnicity, clan, or class but to liberty, indictment produces the spur that excites a people to defend and advance "the cause of liberty." This cyclic and systemic quality of the origins of the free peoples is the reason why their freedom is perfect even in the face of the characteristically indefinite knowledge of its origins. The indefiniteness effects that infuse the political thinking and mindset of the free peoples perfect their kind of life. They continually require proto-freedom and anti-freedom, no matter whether the former is an historical hypothesis or intuition and no matter whether the latter is King George III or terrorism.[14] What does matter is that such effects be modulated at just the right valences, otherwise freedom and the peoples that subscribe to it would be impossible.[15]

The results of this study can now be listed in summary fashion. The idea of peoples at stake in this book have been derived from the *high liberty* or liberal tradition of political writing because that is the literature in which liberty is developed as society's paramount value (rather than any other value such as fairness, equality, knowledge, happiness, etc.). Two effects are necessary for the subscribers to high liberty to originate or to be possible. Its opening instantiation has to be projected as a hazy version of what is to come. And its threats have to be produced as those who, for whatever reason, are against such freedom or against those people who are free. Because precisely these effects are always necessary for it, freedom is the *recurrence of its necessary effects*.[16] It originates in the same way in thought, in the body politic, or in the pages of a book. Freedom is never "a theory" that is then applied "out there" in the "real world." So long as its origins are underway—that is, as long as the practices of synedoche and indictment are working—this familiar, high mode of freedom is effected. If synecdoche or indictment sound too unusual as practices of freedom, they can be translated into more familiar terms. For instance, in his study of De Tocqueville, Pope states that the "sources of freedom" are community associations, the press, decentralized administration, and authoritative laws.[17] But in terms of origins this list of sources translates into those institutions that produce and refine proto-freedom and anti-freedom, especially when such community associations exercise their rights, celebrate their independence, when the press identifies current threats for the public, and when government institutions determine and certify these effects in the courts and the official record.

For the sake of clarification these findings can be related to an international question of concern, namely, the "mission of liberation." The recurring and apparently attractive idea that a people with no explicit history of freedom can be liberated is theoretically correct but would require the expenditure of incredible energies. Simply put, as long as the origination practices that have been noted so far are underway then freedom is produced. Thus if the past of any people, even a previously unfree people, is constructed as free through exhibitions in their museums, in holiday celebrations, in school lessons, in history textbooks, in lectures, in paeans, and in political speeches, then the stage is set for the future advancement of their freedom. Indeed, the very indefiniteness of the origins of free peoples is precisely what allows the persistent idea of the liberation of a people who might otherwise seem patently non-free. Hence, even if the origins of a people's freedom do not have clear historical precedent, then all the better for their induction into the ranks of the free with its typically and necessarily indefinite origins. And so too if threats to a newly freed people are identified as such rather than as threats to party, ethnicity, or to religious dignity by their press, courts, police, and their leadership, then their initially hazy status as free is better secured and solidified as they begin to defend themselves against anti-freedom, perhaps with a revolution.

But there is an important caveat to this tempting renovation of a previously non-free people. The origins of free peoples must not cease. In the political physics of high liberty, entropy is not permitted. Both synedoche and indictment are continuously necessary for a free people to originate and to be maintained. Unfortunately, these practices are precise, even delicate ones. The modulation of both freedom's past and its present require an institutional specialization that is quite technical because the valences required are so exact. For example, the history of a people cannot be so different and definite such that there is no prior freedom in place to be advanced. It is possible, I suppose, for the history of a nonfree people to be appropriately substituted. But such an action would likely be so violent that it would then upset the other, necessarily precise modulation that the threat of anti-freedom requires. In this regard, one could suggest a caveat for what Patrick Henry said about the relation between liberty and death. What he meant was: "give me liberty or" the possibility of "death" because a people faced with certain death will never opt for freedom. The threat to a people cannot be so varied or so unremitting as to make survival into the more important priority than freedom.

The last point to make in this brief diagnosis of the "liberation" mission is that the practices deployed for liberty to originate must predominate in a society for it to be classified as free. They must suffuse it. Otherwise the origins of free peoples will be drowned out by other practices attempting to produce other effects (and other peoples). The liberation of others is not a one-time public-relations matter of winning hearts and minds. It is much harder than that, for it is a matter of hegemonically and continually calibrating a people's history and their threats.

Perfecting the Past

Ambiguity has often been viewed as a problem in the modern tradition of political philosophy rather than as a solution. In terms of thought or expression, ambiguity is typically seen as a deficiency in the same way that one might need further study because one was not yet ready for a spelling contest. But it does not have to be so. In the field of engineering, ambiguity is built into blueprints in the form of tolerances that relieve anticipated stresses or loads on bridges or other superstructures. So too has it been for the builders of freedom although they have been less willing to own up to it. Note, for example, Locke's explanation for such a deficiency, this one in political history and "memory." Thus:

> Government is every where antecedent to Records, and Letters seldome come in amongst a People, till a long continuation of Civil Society has, by other more necessary Arts provided for their Safety, Ease, and Plenty. And then they will begin to look after the History of their *Founders*, and search into their *original*, when they have out-lived the memory of it. (Locke II, §101)

The idea that by the time that historical records can be kept it is too late to record the origins of society is, on the face of it, a sensible enough explanation for why such origins are hazy. But imagine if such poor "memory" were beneficial, even productive? Suppose further that some forgetfulness were the only way that a particular kind of political order, perhaps a Lockean sort, could originate? Then, reproducing such deficiency would not signal a historical inevitability so much as perfect that politics.

It would certainly be easy enough to react against the indefiniteness that is repeatedly found in the chronicles of the free peoples by demanding clarity or coherence. But to do so would mean to strive for a standard of rationality or argumentative elegance instead of what is standard for the kind of people who esteem liberty as paramount. For example, in the chronicles of free peoples it always seems that some bit of the freedom to emerge later in the account has already originated. The famous writings of Locke or Jefferson start with the suggestion that a free people, upon becoming threatened, fought to better secure their liberty because they found it useful. Contemporary philosophers of liberty advance similarly by noting that a "free personality," in encountering deficiencies, seeks to clarify or advance their initial intuitions because freedom is important for what Swanton calls "human flourishing." This familiar pattern and chronology of advancement was called in the introductory chapter of this book the usefulness thesis of origins. Of course, such explanations continue to beg the question of origins since the freedom of the protagonists is always already in place. No doubt some social science rule of hypothesis testing is violated when the freedom that is said to emerge because of its usefulness had already emerged. In his study of another such usefulness thesis, Nietzsche noted not a scientific absurdity but a "psychological absurdity" that seems to apply to all such arguments for origins.[18] To wit, if the origins of freedom come from the fact that it is found so helpful to human flourishing then "why can't those origins be remembered?" Why all the hazy opening hypotheses of intuitions, F-phenomena, states of nature, and self-evident truths? Did the beloved freedom of the people drop its usefulness somewhere along the way? Was it for a brief moment in the past thought not to be useful resulting in an unrecoverable memory loss? But nothing is more certain and certified today by history, rationality, and common sensibilities than the indispensability of liberty.

Nietzsche never followed up on the absurdities of usefulness theses of origins as a basis for criticism and wisely so. He seems to have brought them up only to assure his readers that he had not overlooked them. And so also has it been brought up here, in order to emphasize that the consistency or coherence of a theory of freedom is not the first priority, in spite of strenuous efforts in this direction by contemporary philosophers. Many a critic has floundered challenging initial instantiations such as states of nature or intuitions as impossibilities or falsehoods, no doubt to the secret glee of their proponents. In *The Anarchy*, written in the early seventeenth century, Sir Robert Filmer was perhaps the first and most incredulous critic in this respect. In the case of social contract theories of origins, as those theories of political origins that typically begin with a state of nature, Filmer could not find a time in recorded history when "the people" had inaugurated government and thereby guaranteed their "natural liberty." It was also difficult to tell which naturally free "people" had managed to do this, this section of them, that one, or the whole? But these and similar criticisms, however empirically reasonable, fell on deaf ears. "'Tis often asked as a mighty Objection, *Where are*, or ever were, *any Men in such a state of Nature?*"[19] Along a similar but updated vein, Norman admits that no aspect of Anglo-American political philosophy (which he calls "methodological Rawlsianism") has received more criticism than its starting point of "intuitions."[20] These are not my intuitions, it could be contended; so whose are we talking about and why just this or that collocation of them? Such criticisms, notes Norman, are never a bother because "moral philosophers are invited to continue the search for non-intuitionist foundations, but methodological Rawlsians will proceed with strategies designed to convert opponents who they assume do not, in fact, share such foundational beliefs." It would seem then that the "foundationalism" of arguments for origins is not of concern for Locke, Nietzsche, or for anyone else.

This near unanimous dismissal of foundations or what Baudrillard calls the murder of reality is understandable here because the first priority of a free people is neither rational foundations nor coherence but only their freedom and what is needed for it.[21] And the first task in this regard is that a fraction of their freedom be projected as prior so that at least some bit is around to be threatened and thereby enable its full advancement. A fraction of the freedom to come is therefore necessary philosophically, as when Benn carefully tracks the transition from his opening instance of freedom, the "natural personality," to full-scale "freedom as autarchy." It is also necessary historically as in the drive from Patterson's crude slaveholding societies (but already freedom-wishing ones) to the citizen-republics of ancient Athens or Rome. The self-evidence of liberty in Jefferson's *Declaration* too is no mere rhetorical flourish because precisely such an underconceptualized precondition is pivotal. How else could there be an American liberty to be advanced by patriotic rebellion if there were not already some bit of their same liberty around in the first place? Connolly raises the point when he takes issue with Kateb over the latter's characterization of early nineteenth-century America as an age of innocent freedom. Connolly notes "the past ain't what it used to be. What's more, it probably never was."[22] Indeed, what is most important for free peoples is not the accuracy of the history but its effect. They may or may not live in an era after innocence (or after virtue). They may or may not actually be born free and that may or may not be self-evident. What is crucial is that at least some bit of that happy, free past is required for the fuller emergence of a free people. So somebody better put that precondition into place with an ideological pamphlet, with a work of philosophy or, in Jefferson's case, with a grand declaration. When taken seriously, therefore, the usual hazy interpretations of freedom's past are not the best (or worse) guesses about the history of free peoples so much as what is best for their possibility. In his *Declarations of Independence*, Derrida addresses the worth of just such ambiguity. Thus,

> [i]s it that the good people have already freed themselves in fact and are only stating the fact of this emancipation in the Declaration? Or is it rather that they free themselves at the instant of and by the signature of this Declaration? It is not a question of an obscurity or of a difficulty of interpretation, of a problematic on the way to its (re)solution. . . . This obscurity, this undecidability between, let's say, a performative structure and a constative structure, is *required* in order to produce the sought after effect. It is essential to the very positing or position of a right as such.[23]

From the philosophical standpoint of clear argumentation, every proto-freedom that has ever been postulated, from Locke's early modern state of nature to the interpretation of a "good people" who declare their full independence to Swanton's background theory of freedom might be considered poorly conceptualized. But in terms of what is imperative for the origins of a free people, such ambivalence or "undecidability" is perfect.[24] That way, the advancement of their liberty becomes possible because there was at least some of it already lying about.

But there is even more to the chronicle of free peoples because it is not enough that a fraction of their freedom is prior, whether as a "background theory" (Swanton), a "belief structure" (Benn), in the hopes of slaves (Patterson, Kojeve), in the thoughts of peasants (Mackinnon), or in the power calculations of elites (Rogowski). Such fractional freedom also has to be, like Goldilocks porridge, just right. As I have noted, if the opening instance of freedom in the chronicle of origins were too well conceptualized or too well understood, there would be no need for freedom to originate (more fully because of its usefulness). A rebellion by a free people in order to advance their cause would then be unwarranted. On the other hand, if the freedom beforehand were too underformulated, freedom would then be too faint to come under threat and, again, there would be no need for it to be advanced (more fully). For the student of origins, the requirement of such precise modulation adds force to the argument that free peoples do not arise by "contingency," "nature," "right," or desert but only by way of practical, political, and all-too-human origins.

Of course the idea that we are born free or that freedom is self-evident is profound and deeply ingrained. "The origins of freedom?" a colleague once quipped, "never thought much about it." It is no easy undertaking to dislodge the comfortable and hazy history of free peoples in favor of their frenetic if mundane origins. But the task begins with radical thought and the refusal to stop thinking in political terms; that is, it begins with a refusal to stop making concrete connections, a refusal to stop providing reasons, and a refusal to stop arguing politically. In his quest for the liberation of the Ghanaian people, Nkrumah counseled, "seek ye first the political kingdom." Chapter 2 of this book on prerevolutionary liberty was instrumental in this regard because it illustrated the imperative of effecting the past of free peoples just right. It did so because that past was, admittedly, produced quite wrongly for the task at hand. Not only are Filmer, Astell, De Maistre, and the American Loyalists not the first thinkers to come to mind in the history of free peoples, but their notion of liberty as royal grant is dissimilar to what was to predominate later in the history of Western political thought. Indeed, those absolutist writers are more likely to be found in a history of antiliberty, or "antiliberalism" to use Holmes's term, if not as precursors to totalitarianism.[25] But it was precisely the dissimilarity of their liberty that raised the question of origins. After all, it is a rather standard trope in the history of political thought to raise such figures from oblivion and claim that they have been unfairly neglected. Why then have these writers been firmly rejected for the history of liberty and indeed why should they be rejected?—for the best of political reasons because their dissimilar liberty interferes with what is imperative for the origins of free peoples today. The celebrated chronicle of freedom, threat, and advancement is not possible if there is not at least a fraction of the *same* freedom in place prior to the revolution that more fully secures it.

Thus, to dislodge comfortable historical notions of origins, this book began with a wrong history of the free peoples in order to force thinking about precisely what would be needed in their history for it to be right.

Beginning the history of liberty with the prerevolutionary version as royal grant made origins, for a change, into an urgent concern and question. It did so because seeing Filmer's or De Maistre's strange versions of liberty as the opening and prior freedom in the history of free peoples forces the reader toward a complete recollection of what is imperative for *their* freedom. That dissimilar history was provocative in the same way that a challenger besmirches the honor of a noble opponent and draws him out, enraged, to defend what is proper. As has been noted, most contemporary authors and chroniclers are too casual about the origins of the freedom that they champion, which is why its source is unproblematically described as everything from a natural, divine, or contingent endowment, to a self-evident truth, to a collection of intuitions. It seems to be enough that proto-freedom and the proto-free simply popped up, like the fanciful men-mushrooms of Hobbes's *De Cive*.[26] Proto-freedom may even be explicitly downplayed, as in the case of one contemporary thinker whose original position, the "background theory of freedom," is said to be merely a device that "helps us make progress" in our understanding of freedom. But no matter how indifferent and nonreflexive, contemporary commentators on liberty are always sure to do their history properly and place a similar fraction of the freedom to come in their chronicles. Only in that way can they get back to the future of their freedom. It is likely that little notice would be taken of their quite right historical writing and thinking if it had not been done so wrong in this book. The interpretation of prerevolutionary liberty in Chapter 2 was a kind of old-fashioned test of the null hypothesis. Behavioral scientists stopped using that test by the 1980s because they thought that it yielded only trivial results. But in this case, confirming the hypothesis that a dissimilar freedom as prior does not allow for a free people serves to recall that only a similar, prior form will do. That, of course, is the whole point: to recall how free peoples must originate.

It is not clear if, in spite of this originary imperative, a state of nature like Swanton's "background theory" is downplayed as a mere "device" because a similar liberty in the past can be taken for granted as an "obvious" fact of human history. For example, even careful philosophical writers sometimes make claims to the empirical status of their intuitive, opening, free states (e.g., Swanton's background theory as an "empirical hypothesis" or Benn's "natural" personality).[27] This kind of claim to factuality is not uncommon and is worth some address, but one has to be careful how it is addressed. First, following Nietzsche's lesson that logical absurdities in usefulness theses of origins are to be ignored, it is unwise to try to determine the historical status, if any, of any state of nature. The student of origins does not wish to wind up like Filmer, fruitlessly exclaiming that no such state has ever existed in human history. Indeed, the controversy over the exact status of Locke's initially free state still rages centuries later. Simmons muses, "[i]s the state of nature a historical period that preceded governments?[28] Or is it the state into which every person, even today, is born? Or is it simply an analytical device used by Locke to justify civil society, a convenient fiction with no actual historical instantiations?" Frankly, these questions about historical accuracy or authorial intention pale next to the immediately practical and less complicated question of whether Locke's free people could originate without some such state? The answer of course is that they could not do so.

If our contemporary authors do believe that their history of liberty can be taken for granted as an empirical fact "out there," which intuitions or a background theory only reflect, then beginning that history with Astell's or Filmer's equally empirical liberty undercuts that assurance because it becomes evident that, again, not just any history will do but only the right one. That is why, of all political writers who could have been brought in to begin this study of origins, prerevolutionary thinkers such as Filmer or De Maistre remain important to a consideration of free peoples of today. They may be the wrong thinkers to reference for such a history, but they help to recall that the origins of free peoples must be done perfectly not accurately. The history of every free people is always biased. This is not because, as some crestfallen writers and cynics have said, everything is relative in a postmodern or even a post-postmodern age. It is because the effect of proto-freedom has to be just right otherwise the sort of free people that have been in question here would not be possible.

The field of history is just as sure a bet as the field of philosophy when it comes to ensuring that the past of the free peoples is perfect. To be sure, the historians' reliance upon archival documents or other evidence is often meant to reinforce their claims to a verifiable view of the past. Historians have not been idle in the face of what they have come to see as forceful "relativist" challenges to their objectivity. They have become cagier of late and have begun to speak of history, and the history of liberty, as less linear and more complicated, even priding themselves on producing pastiche histories.[29] For example, Appleby concedes, "the word 'freedom' always looks the same even though its import has varied drastically over the centuries—the historical text should be addressed as a puzzle."[30] It used to be enough for the historian to point to a steady string of early peasant or other rebellions, from the premodern era onward, to trace the "origins" and linear "progress" of liberty toward the familiar modern stage of full "political rights."[31] Today, historians are more modest and more reflexive because of the "puzzle" or complexity of history and the acknowledged difficulties of historiography. However, when historians suggest that the emergence of modern freedom was a complex affair, this means very little for the specific possibility of the free peoples because what is imperative has changed not one iota. High liberty still requires a fraction to be set in the past for it to be better secured by reform or revolution. As long as this imperative is fulfilled, even if the effect has become harder to discern because history is now more puzzling, free peoples are enabled. The complexity of history sounds like a welcome admission on the part of many scholars, as though they are acknowledging the commonsense idea that life is not simple. But such complexity (as well as such commonsense) can nonetheless contain a postulation with important political and practical implications because proto-freedom can be embedded in the "puzzle" of the past and once more allow for the free peoples to originate and advance.

Exactly how faded the historical memory of a free people can become and still enable the maintenance of their liberty is a somewhat interesting practical and increasingly popular question. For example, Huntington's book on the contemporary American identity, entitled *Who are We?*, highlights the question of how the way that the history of the American people is written determines their prospects for the future. Huntington cites a number of other concerns in his book but what is especially relevant to the question of the prospects of his free people is the complaint that American historiography is changing for the worse. According to Huntington, the propagation of the archetypal story of the American founding is fading due to the dilutive effects of immigration (since many immigrants don't know that story), nonassimilation (since such people refuse to embrace that story), and transnationalism (because it is then one story among many). The classic story of founding is fading in terms of its dignity as "the teaching of national history has given way to the teaching of ethnic and racial histories." The latter histories, thinks Huntington, tend to impute the American historical experience as one not of freedom but of injustice, hypocrisy, and even cruelty. Huntington's book seems to echo cyclical concerns that come and go throughout American history about new immigrants, about their patriotism, and about their civic education and integration.

The one concern of Huntington's that the student of origins can dispel is his problem of the fading history of the American founding. If we measure what has been typically pronounced as prior to the full emergence of a free people, it appears that proto-freedom can become quite faded and still enable its celebrated benefits. It is not clear if this claim can be quantified, but the various chronicles that have been noted presented examples of proto-freedom that would strain our eyesight, if not our credulity, were we to try to find empirical examples of them. The wispy intuitions of the philosophers' freedom, Jefferson's parsimonious self-evidence of liberty, and Locke's relatively few chapters on the state of nature seem to me to be far sketchier and less tangible than the graves of Huntington's heroes of the American revolution and the gleaming neoclassical monuments that have been erected in their honor. The additional histories of freedom developed in "ethnic studies" or uncovered by feminists as well as other groups only add to the brisk air of liberty. Many of them determine proto-freedom and anti-freedom also, albeit differently. Proto-freedom does not only have to mean Plymouth Rock and anti-freedom does not only have to be King George. Thus, if Huntington is worried about the future of Americans' freedom (which is perhaps the main element of their "identity"), then he need not yet be concerned.

Ultimately, the conclusion to be drawn is simply that the indefinite past of freedom and those people that subscribe to it must be perfect. This is not an idealistic but a practical conclusion for only a specific technique can be expected to replicate precisely what is imperative. The opening instantiation of a free people has to be modulated to the perfect valence of ambiguousness. Their proto-freedom has to be indefinite but not so thinly that it cannot become credibly threatened. But it also cannot be so thickly formulated that its advancement to more of the same kind of freedom is unwarranted (e.g., more secure freedom in the familiar guise of civil and political liberties guaranteed by limited government). Such perfect modulation cannot depend for long upon historical contingency or the self-evident truth of men's liberty as endowed by heaven. The fortunate blessings of deity yesterday may not enable what is needed today. The same caveat holds for the flighty intuitions of the philosophers since a collocation of our intuitions today may not be the same tomorrow. Freedom can however rely on "intuitions," "contingency," or "divine" endowments as a function of their repeated postulation or, more simply, as the effect of particular actions taken that, when reiterated, reproduce exactly what is needed. By reiterating such perfect underformulations in turn, the student of origins not only puts forth what is necessary for that liberty but also what serves as a proof of the study of its origins, namely, practices that, if replicated, effect what is recognizable as the political life of free society.

Perfecting the Present

Sadly there are few good explanations for why at least a few of Locke's individuals turn up with a "settled design" on the natural liberty of their fellows. If there were, a policy solution could be prescribed for the problem and a much happier present could be experienced. Instead it is all somewhat inexplicable, which is perhaps reason enough and explains why one can kill those who threaten freedom as if they were "a Wolf or a Lyon."[32] The usual explanations for the origins of such threats proceed little further than descriptions suggesting that the injurer made a poor choice or did not see fit to consult the laws of nature that govern the opening state of liberty. And the persistence of such threats, beyond Locke's day and beyond his state of war, is commonly ascribed to the "imperfection" of humanity or the world. Other than the descriptive and tautological explanation that bad choices are made by bad individuals or that they were beings who exercised their liberty defectively, the exact origins of such threats remain a mystery. The explanations given, such as they are, beg the question of the origins of threats to freedom. But in following the trail of such fitful logic, the lack of explanation of origins turns out not to be a major concern compared to the overriding perception that what is cherished has become threatened. "Who cares how it got there?" one might hear. "What is to be done about it?"[33] As Pettit states plainly in his *Freedom as Anti-power*, "historical context is more or less irrelevant to whether domination occurs in a relation . . ."[34] Pettit goes on to insist that the "salient question" is simply how to stop the threat of domination. Evidently then, the origins of domination are not the priority in this case.

Instead, I argue that the reason for this lack of curiosity is because free peoples, their commentators included, do quite well under uninvestigated conditions of threat. The imperfect mode of freedom would not be possible if the origins of a threat like domination were unambiguous. This is why Pettit does not care how the "salient" problem of "domination" arises and also why fellow contemporary thinkers such as Benn or Swanton never ask how their various "deficiencies" or "flaws" of freedom originate. After all, threats to freedom, which always seem to occupy the present of free peoples in some form or other, have never overwhelmed the free world because they were not understood well enough. Indeed, the simplistic view that anti-freedom emerges from an "imperfect world" has not only not stopped the free peoples. Rather, just such ambivalence, clearly threatening *and* without a clear understanding of how it is so, has been perfect for them. They have flourished in precisely such misunderstood times.

Nevertheless, that even the vague understanding of the origins of anti-freedom still has a quite specific valence can be seen if one imagines that valence set at different and wrong modulations. For example, if the threat to a free people were not "salient" but rather merely annoying, then the defense and advancement of their freedom in the form of revolution or resistance would not arise as the expected response. Rather, free peoples would more likely ignore such a minor threat and continue to inhabit their innocent, prepolitical utopias or natural states. Anti-freedom provides the rationale for the full-scale origination of a free people, but it must have a level of palpability beyond what Baudrillard once called "irritation."[35] Enmity, not mere alterity, is what is required in this regard. Recall how Locke (II, §8) was not satisfied simply with the threat that derived solely from a "transgression of the Law of Nature." A violation or transgression of that law, by itself, did not carry enough weight to advance his liberty further. But that ineffective valence was transformed once Locke's "Offender" makes a self-declaration to be a "danger to Mankind" and a "Noxious creature." The threshold of anti-freedom was then reached with this clear charge of threat. This was because by itself a legal "transgression" is a rather boring technical matter to be interpreted by attorneys or bureaucrats. But the added charge of being a "danger to Mankind" and a "Noxious creature" cannot be set aside for careful juridical analysis later. Nor can much time be spared to determine the veracity of the charges. The first response has to be to defend and secure one's liberty against the threat. Furthermore, given the new weight of the threat, one no longer has to be an expert in natural or positive law to recognize what is at stake. Everything and everyone in a free society is then under threat. As Locke put it, "he that in the State of Society, would take away the *Freedom* belonging to those of that Society or Common-wealth, must be supposed to design to take away from them everything else."

But if the threat of anti-freedom cannot be too weak, it also cannot be too strong. For example, if the world were outright wicked or even if only part of it were, that is, if there were as much right to evil as to good as with the old Manichean universe, then the advancement of freedom would again not be the automatic response. Collaboration, appeasement, or stoicism rather than any spirited defense of liberty would be responses in a dualistic world where the anti-free had an equally rightful stronghold. The example of Augustine is instructive in this regard. When Augustine turned away from and eventually upon his youthful Manicheanism, he did so by implicating all of mankind in imperfection.[36] The old distinction where the good and the evil each had their own rightful place in the moral universe disappeared. What is interesting is that such a transformation does not do away with the good or the perfect (for how could Augustine do away with his god?). It only makes goodness into the single standard that should be striven for by all and, by the same token, makes those who do not strive toward it accountable for their deficiency. Thanks to the Augustinian transfiguration, all of humanity became less than perfectly good, which was not the case in the old, dualistic universe in which one could also be classified as less than perfectly evil.

Anti-freedom also originates only in a post-Augustinian, less than perfectly moral world. But contrary to what some contemporary thinkers believe, their realist, "pragmatic," and "commonsensical" admissions that the world is "imperfect" do not do away with "idealism." Instead, unattainable perfection simply becomes the unseen, singular, standard against which everyone is to be measured. For example, Raphael states, "[t]he norm of natural choices and desires that we take as a standard in our concept of freedom is not a 'higher' or 'best' self, as the Idealists suggest, but is the natural character of an average human being in normal circumstances."[37] As commonsensical as this assessment sounds however, Raphael's "average" or "normal" standard carries an additional, idealistic standard secretly in tow. The free, whether Locke's, Benn's, Swanton's, or Raphael's, will admittedly never arrive at perfect liberty. According to Locke's account, free people exit their state of "perfect freedom" almost as soon as it is mentioned. But even though such perfection is out of reach, they can at least be given credit, imperfect beasts that they are, for striving for what is morally right. And of course, to continue this classic tale, those who choose to become threats to freedom will be held accountable for their acts since they are then struggling against the one and only standard that they should be striving toward. To be sure, if this account were Manichean then such threatening beings would still rate poorly when measured against the standard of perfect liberty. But they would also rate highly when measured against the other standard that sits across the way. In the post-Augustinian world however the latter pole as an equal moral standard has disappeared. Under this scheme, all free peoples are implicated in political and moral imperfection. And it is only in such a scheme that those who are identified as threats can be found to have violated the one and only "natural law" of freedom.

The point to be drawn is, once more, that anti-freedom has to be per-fectly modulated for the origins of free people. If the threat were too powerful, then that recalls Manicheanism, which would confuse the moral classification of threats to freedom. An injurer could then still be deemed as against anti-free, but it would also be natural for him to be so. The latter reading is not possible, however, in the modern scheme. Note, for example, how carefully Kant calibrates modern "evil," even when he calls it "radical." Hence,

> there is in man a natural propensity to evil; and since this very propensity must in the end be sought in a will, which is free, and can therefore be imputed, it is morally evil. This evil is radical because it corrupts the ground of all maxims; it is, moreover, as a natural propensity, inextirpable by human powers, since extirpation could only occur through good maxims, and cannot take place when the ultimate subjective ground of all maxims is postulated as corrupt; yet at the same time it must be possible to overcome it, since it is found in man, a being whose actions are free.[38]

It is not possible to completely "extirpate" threats to freedom (hence such evil is always in our present: on the nightly news, in church sermons, in new philosophical publications on freedom, etc.). Extirpation would presuppose purely good maxims and these are not available when the "ultimate subjective ground of all maxims" is "corrupt" or imperfect. The broad diffusion of corruption is the reason why "evil" is fairly powerful for Kant, even "radical." Nevertheless it is not so fundamental that it cannot be "overcome" by the free, for if it were so basic, then the ultimate subjective ground of maxims would be worse than just "corrupt." In term of freedom's origins, anti-freedom must come in just the right valence otherwise it would not be possible, as it evidently must be for Kant's free man to "overcome" it. What this requirement means practically and politically is that Kant's free men cannot depend upon humanity to always be "corrupt" in just the right valence. The post-Augustinian and neo-Kantian belief that the world or humankind is "imperfect," while it may today be filled with evidence to that effect, may not be enough tomorrow because a particular sort of free people is at stake, which always requires perfect imperfection. Indeed, the natural corruption or imperfection of mankind would seem to be the last source that anyone should count on to regularly send along the exact valence of threat needed for free peoples.

In contrast, therefore, to Kant and to those neo-Kantian authors who attribute the origins of "evil" to an imperfect world or humanity "out there," the student of origins rewrites and thus reproduces the effect of injury, crime, or other threat to freedom, thereby recalling that claims that the world are "imperfect" are slanders against humanity rather than facts about it.

Note, however, that just this kind of production of anti-freedom or evil as "positivity" is what Kant will not admit. To again follow his thinking:

> We are not then to call the depravity of human nature *wickedness*, taking the word in its strict sense as a disposition (the subjective principle of the maxims) to adopt evil as evil into our maxim as our incentives (for that is diabolical); we should rather term it the *perversity of the heart*, which, then, because of what follows from it, is also called an *evil heart* . . . Such a heart may co-exist with a will which in general is good: it arises from the frailty of human nature, the lack of sufficient strength to follow out the principles it has chosen for itself, joined with its impurity, the failure to distinguish the incentives (even of well-intentioned actions) from each other by the gauge of morality.[39]

Kant would rather term what is evil "perversity"—that is, to lack, failure, deficiency, or something that falls short of a single standard (according to the "gauge of morality")— than to rate it against another equal principle for evil. One can certainly empathize with Kant's preference because the stakes involved are high. It is one thing to speak of a disposition for freedom, which is an absolute good but which may be practiced imperfectly. But it is but quite another matter to also speak of a disposition for anti-freedom. Kant's "radical evil" would not then result from the lamentable "failure" of trying to be free. It would derive instead from the "diabolical" effort of attempting to be anti-free. There would then be two equal guiding principles that free people could follow, one for good and one for evil as in Schelling's neglected definition of "freedom" as "a possibility of good *and* evil."[40]

As much as Kant might wish his free humanity to be potentially innocent, if imperfect, in practice, it is their own mode of freedom that betrays his desire. When there is a new threat for a free people to worry about, the reason behind it is not because ultimately, "nobody's perfect." Nor is the reason the even more nebulous because "they hate our freedoms."[41] Rather it is because the production of such threats has always been an integral part of what such freedom entails (hence the deployment of the term anti-freedom). As Coole put it, "the nature of the externality of impediments thus becomes highly problematic."[42] "Perversity," "power," or other "impediments" to the free do not simply pop up from the world "out there," say, because man is naturally that way at bottom (e.g., less than perfect or "corrupt") and so it is simply to be expected. Rather, such threats, indeed such humans, have to be continually constructed as such. This is because there is no other way to guarantee exactly what is needed for free peoples all of the time other than to have institutions in place that reproduce it. To be sure, much of the contemporary discussion of liberty centers on security, preservation, and guarantees. Indeed, Bentham rather nicely defined freedom as security.[43] But it is because such peculiar freedom can advance only with a precise valence of threat that anti-freedom must be a produced effect. Such ongoing and necessary perfection is why threats to freedom are not exogenous to its origins. Crime, injury, or terrorism as threats to freedom are all very specific effects. Much work, economic, political, social, and philosophical, has to be done to have their origins not be understood too well.

Specifically it is only by leveling a charge that he or she is a threat to liberty, is "criminal," is "psychotic," is "schizophrenic," or is "irrational" that anti-freedom can originate. Then, like the imperfect world that he is said to spew from, the anti-free being is produced perfectly as both threatening *and* as uncertain as to how he became so. Indictment is necessarily endogenous to the liberty ecology, for only then can anti-freedom be the "salient" problem of a free people. It becomes impossible to "extirpate" such threats because little can be done about its natural, if mysterious, roots in corruption or human imperfection. Instead, as the Kantians would argue (and perhaps the majority of liberal theorists today are Kantians), anti-freedom must be overcome practically through the advancement and defense of freedom with acts and institutions that secure a free people against their threats. But for this to happen, anti-freedom must be just right. If it were too well understood, free peoples might finally solve or live with the problem rather than repeatedly try to overcome it. But if it were too little known, there would then be no threat worth worrying about.

What can be concluded, therefore, is that just as the free peoples must produce precisely the right past for their liberty, so also must they produce just the right present, be that the imperfect world or those imperfect humans who regularly solidify in some form or other to threaten them. Anti-freedom or threats to freedom must be produced effects because their valence must be perfectly modulated, not too wicked and not just annoying. Only then are they just the right effect needed for this mode of freedom. As such, they also require just the right productive practice. Unfortunately, indictment, as a form of prosecution or accusation, is that practice. Perhaps nothing produces the anti-free effect better (as a threat that is obviously present *and* unclear how it became so) than the simple gesture of pointing an accusing finger. Ostracism used to be the punishment of choice for citizens of another, more ancient, free society. But today's free societies cannot let their enemies go, in the same way that victims of traumatic stress syndrome complain about but repeatedly replay their worst experiences. Free societies today are fascinated by their threats from their inception and for their continued origination. If threats like "Sir Robert" or "King George III" were the spur for the advancement of such freedom in the first place, why would such a spur not still be necessary today? As Jefferson once noted, the "tree of liberty must be refreshed from time to time with the blood of patriots and tyrants." Freedom is not a "thing" once gained and then defended but is always a "hatching."[44] It should come as no surprise that institutions have formed to continuously find, reproduce, and refine what is imperative for it.

If free peoples require anti-freedom for their full origination, then it will come as no surprise to find institutions dedicated to the development of such threats. But also since that threat is often presumed to arise from the "simple fact" of a dangerous world "out there," these institutions can appear to have other, unrelated purposes. For example, "[m]odern penalty depoliticizes crime; it draws attention to the character of the criminal and away from the power of the regime."[45] The key to the decryption of institutional practices in this case is to remain focused on what is imperative for freedom (rather than for power). For instance, the criminal justice system today provides a setting for restorative justice, but the way that its institutions address suspects *also* makes it a venue for the refinement of antifreedom.[46] In those societies that claim freedom as their paramount value, their criminal justice systems are remarkable for how steadily they repeat their accusations. In a fearsome mirror image of the philosophical catalogs of flaws of freedom, the criminal justice system is also a system that repeats its charges from the moment a suspect is first identified to each day that he stews behind bars as what he is said to be. "For the observation that the prison fails to eliminate crime, one should perhaps substitute the hypothesis that prison has succeeded extremely well in producing delinquency, of a specific type."[47] Where dungeons were places where bodies wasted away and gulags have been where bodies are excited beyond their capacity to recover, the penitentiary keeps bodies static and, as Foucault showed, rigorously "disciplined" as "delinquents." Each day, for his specified time, the antifree individual is charged as such once more. If it were possible, it would be advantageous if he did not physically age while "doing his time" so as to freeze him that way as in the film *Demolition Man*.

What Foucault once notoriously characterized as the "carceral society" was more precisely the *prosecutorial society* because incarceration or imprisonment is merely the most physical mode of accusation. It is perhaps worth noting here that in the history of juridical accusation, ancient Athenian prosecutors could face extremely serious penalties, including banishment or crippling fines, if they lost their cases. No longer. It is a measure of the demands of a new, and quite different, free people that such safeguards have been drastically lessened. That one accused might be found innocent at trial is very much an important point, legally and ethically. But what is imperative for freedom to originate (and that is the sole focus of this study, not justice nor any other value) is that the charge be made and that some anti-freedom is thereby present and accounted for.[48] If this or that body is no longer charged as anti-free because he is found not guilty in a court or by the latest DNA test, the prosecutorial apparatus will continue its activity elsewhere and that activity, no matter how it is deployed intentionally or consciously, does not seek truth but only anti-freedom.

Ultimately, to address the origins of free peoples means to put the naturalistic view of their freedom as simply already around into question not as falsehood but as a social science challenge of figuring out practically how that happens. To address these origins practically is also to become aware of why the hazy, naturalistic view has had such a thrall, even for clear-headed philosophers. It is because such origins are not ambiguous or indefinite by themselves. Rather, powerful sociopolitical processes are underway to construct them because free peoples, as they have so far been known, are at stake. This study has been an attempt to draw out those productive processes but not for the sake of philosophical curiosity. Because the originating processes have so much continual force and impact it is likely that some free people have already become aware of them, even worried by them. It is this growing band of committed free people, sensitized to their origins, who may steer what has been their usual past and present toward some brighter future to be outlined in the epilogue.

Notes

1. The idea of indefinite political knowledge or "imperfect information" is a familiar one in political science but, in contrast to the theory of the origins of free peoples, it brings in tow with it a caste distinction between those "in the know" and those in ignorance. The classic expression is Downs's *Economic Theory of Democracy*. For Downs, imperfect information is the key to political, especially voter, behavior. Trying to understand politics is costly and so the decision to remain ignorant on the part of the citizen is rational. Nonvoting is rational behavior too since the lack of information makes the choice between political candidates undifferentiated. In terms of political power, the overall result is that the various

players depend upon information proprietors in order to successfully participate. Citizens turn to parties and interest groups to gather and provide them with political information. Candidates and representatives do the same in order to discern what constituents want. In political theory, the issue of imperfect political knowledge is not axiomatic so much as deliberate on the part of intellectuals "in the know" that practice esotericism. Metaphorically speaking, the difference between the "city" and "philosophy" is too great to bridge and so political philosophers must offer customary platitudes to the public even though their own analyses may show them to be a sham. In either model, whether the information deficit is a problem of rationality or a deliberate strategy, the political society is split between information elites and information subjects; Calvert, *Models*, 12; Schaefer, "Leo Strauss," 190. By contrast, in the spirit of the Enlightenment and universalism, free peoples as a whole experience the same information deficit or collective amnesia.

2. Constant, *Political*, 307.

3. Harding, "Political," 430.

4. "Today I am signing into law H.R. 4655, the 'Iraq Liberation Act of 1998' . . . The United States favors an Iraq that offers its people freedom at home. I categorically reject arguments that this is unattainable due to Iraq's history or its ethnic or sectarian make-up. Iraqis deserve and desire freedom like everyone else." Clinton, "Statement," 2210.

5. Nancy, *Experience*, 9.

6. "Forgetting is no mere *vis inertiae* as the superficial imagine; it is rather an active and in the strictest sense, positive faculty of repression," Nietzsche, *Basic Writings*, 312.

7. Swanton, *Freedom*, 48.

8. Simpson and Jones, *Europe*, 13.

9. "Criminality proceeds from the very nature of humanity itself," Hibbert, *The Roots*, 225.

10. See Heideking, "Image of an English Enemy," 104. Jefferson's initial draft of the *Declaration* is interesting in this regard. In addition to the list of offences found in the final draft, Jefferson tried to include offenses against another American people, namely, slaves. Thus, "he has waged cruel war against human nature itself, violating its most sacred rights of life and liberty in the person of a distant people who never offended him captivating and carrying them into another hemisphere." Jefferson also tried to impugn the British people, not only the king in that draft. However a "few minor changes in his draft were made by Franklin and Adams. Other changes were later made by Congress. The most important of these eliminated Jefferson's condemnation of the slave trade and his censure of the people of Great Britain," Perry, *Sources*, 317. Jefferson thus conceived proto-freedom and anti-freedom quite differently than is popularly thought in his initial draft, a draft which, according to his letter to Adams, Jefferson became depressed about when it was edited. See Derrida, *Declarations*, 8.

11. Zizek, "The Loop," 206; Sallis, "Schelling's System," 156.

12. Their freedom may be conceptualized as the *freedom to not be coerced*. In his seminal lecture, Berlin distinguished freedom into negative and positive forms as "freedom from" and "freedom to" but politically affirmed only the former conception. McCallum later combined Berlin's categories into the formulation of the "freedom of x from y to do z." In terms of their ongoing origins, free peoples are more involved and proactive than Berlin expected and their aims more circumscribed than McCallum predicted for they not only seek freedom from y but the z that they do is to ensure that just the right amount of y is available; Berlin, "Two Concepts," 233; MacCallum, "Negative and Positive," 314.

13. Dillon, *Politics*, 116.

14. "The proof lies in Bentham who simultaneously and consistently developed a political theory of the self-interested subject . . . and techniques for administering the social whole through discipline," Brown, *States of Injury*, 19.

15. "The Perfect needs the Imperfect in order to assert itself. *This is why there is Evil in the World: on account of the perverse need of the Perfect for the Imperfect,*" Zizek, *The Abyss*, 7.

16. For example, the "'Magna Carta being confirmed thirty times, for so often have the kings of England given their royal assents thereunto . . . and the said two charters have been confirmed, established, and commanded to be put into execution by thirty-two several acts of parliament in all' . . . Thanks to Sir Edward Coke everyone is familiar with the many parliamentary confirmations of Magna Carta and the Forest Charter," Thompson, *Magna*, 9.

17. Pope, *Search*, 17–20.

18. Nietzsche, *Basic Writings*, 463.

19. Locke, *Two Treatises*, II §14.

20. Norman, "Inevitable," 286.

21. Baudrillard, *Perfect*, i.

22. Connolly, *Identity/Difference*, 84.

23. Derrida, *Declarations*, 9.

24. Honig, "Declarations," 106.

25. Holmes, *Anatomy*, 13, 193.

26. "Let us return again to the state of nature and consider men as if but even now sprung out of the earth, and suddainly (like Mushrooms) come to full maturity without all kind of engagement to each other," Hobbes *De Cive*, 117.

27. Swanton, *Freedom*, 15; Benn, *A Theory*, 8.

28. Simmons, *Lockean Theory of Rights*, 13.

29. E. Foner, "The Story of American Freedom," lecture series at The Getty Research Institute for the History of Art and the Humanities in Los Angeles, March 16, 1998.

30. Appleby, et al., *Telling the Truth*, 211.

31. Mackinnon, *A History*, 14.

32. Locke, *Two Treatises*, II §16.

33. Bennett verbalizes the kind of pragmatic sentiment that often clouds both political and philosophical understandings of origins. "If we want to eliminate the drug problem, these people say, we must first eliminate the 'root cause' of drugs . . . Twenty-five years ago no one would have suggested that we must first address the root causes of racism before fighting segregation. We fought it, quite correctly, by passing laws against unacceptable conduct. The causes of racism was an interesting question but the moral imperative was to end it as soon as possible and by all reasonable means: education, prevention, the media, and not least of all the law. So too with drugs," William Bennett, "Drug Policy and the Intellectuals," lecture delivered at the Kennedy School of Government, December 11, 1989.

34. Pettit, "Freedom," 585.

35. Baudrillard, *Perfect*, 144. Also see Kennedy, "Culture Wars," 349.

36. Connolly, *Identity/Difference*, 125.

37. Raphael, *Problems*, 122.

38. Kant, *Religion*, 32.

39. Ibid., 32.

40. Schelling, *Philosophical*, 26.

41. Lazar and Lazar, "Discourse," 225.

42. Coole, "Constructing," 90.

43. Neocleous, "Security, Liberty," 140.

44. Nancy, *Experience*, 15–16.

45. Connolly, *Politics and Ambiguity*, 106.

46. "On the origin and the purpose of punishment—two problems that are separate, or ought to be separate . . . the cause of the origin of a thing and its eventual utility, its actual employment . . . lie worlds apart," Nietzsche, *Basic Writings*, 336.

47. Foucault, *Discipline*, 277.

48. "There is no trial to be conducted. Louis is not a culprit; you are not judges . . . You do not have a sentence to pronounce for or against a man; you have a measure of public health to take, an action of national providence to exercise. For if Louis can still be the object of a trial, he can be absolved, he can be innocent—what I am saying, he is presumed to be innocent until he is judged. But if Louis is absolved, if Louis can be presumed innocent, what becomes of the revolution? If Louis is innocent all the defenders of freedom become calumniators," Robespierre, quoted in Klossowski, *Sade*, 56.

6

The Fate of Freedom

In contrast to the question of the future of freedom, which addresses how other peoples, as yet unfree, may become free, the question of the fate of freedom addresses the destiny of those who subscribe to it already as their paramount political value. One practical difference in this regard is between what free peoples must do for others and the more surprising question of what they must do for themselves. For example, Zakaria's *Future of Freedom* is a foreign policy suggestion about how freedom, already secure among the free peoples, can be extended to the rest of the world. He argues for liberty before democracy, for rule of law before elections. This sequence of developments was, Zakaria claims, the historical experience of the Western democracies and so should inform their foreign policy in their contacts with the non-Western world. Zakaria's policy statement counsels that, for a time at least, as yet unfree peoples should live under liberal authoritarians or benevolent autocracies rather than having unrestrained rulers repeatedly "win" elections in "illiberal" democracies.[1] Beginning first with liberty, and its immediate benefits of rule of law and economic freedoms, liberal auto-crats will eventually democratize and permit "free and fair" elections. Liberal democracy, not liberty without democracy nor democracy without liberty, is then the outcome for all countries, developing or advanced. Like Fukuyama, Zakaria takes the already-free peoples as a finished and success-ful model needing only to be properly packaged and exported. Practically, then, to address the future of freedom is mostly to address the future of peoples who do not yet subscribe to freedom as their paramount value.

On the other hand, the question of the fate of freedom addresses the less familiar question of the destiny of the already-free peoples. Because Zakaria (and Fukuyama) are serious in their belief that free peoples have reached the zenith of modern political development, the question of their future need not be posed and indeed cannot be considered as an important question. To address the fate of freedom however cannot presume free peoples as a finished project because they are the product of the right practices and effects driven by enough of their own efforts. So while their origins may be ongoing and satisfactory today they may not continue as frenetically tomorrow. To talk of the fate of the free peoples does not imply that they are, as with so much post-Spengler speculation these days, in decline or near "the end." The "end of history" or "the West" is not a question distinctive to the free peoples and so is uninteresting here (although the fact that this annoying eschatological question arises so often may be worth study). To address the fate of free peoples is also not to suggest that they may dramatically change their policies if by that is meant they will discontinue their ongoing productions of protofreedom and antifreedom. That is impossible so long as freedom remains their paramount value. The fate of free peoples is different, then, from their future, which is primarily a question about their encounters with nonfree peoples, and different from the question of their end, which from the perspective of the political theory of freedom is uninteresting.

The difference in analytic focus between the future and fate of free peoples can be traced to the important presumption that their freedom was already around naturally or intuitively and fully originates because of its usefulness for them. This familiar chronology or account of political development, dubbed here the usefulness thesis of origins, is ultimately why Zakaria, President Bush, and many others can believe unfree peoples will become (fully) free if only obstacles such as autocrats are removed since the natural liberty of the people should then blossom forth. To be sure, the claim that freedom is natural or self-evident is no longer stated explicitly in contemporary political philosophy. These days political liberty is said to be "intuitive" and given the successful socioeconomic model that free peoples are thought to offer, obviously useful. But whether natural or intuitive, the implication is the same since almost any policy action taken to foster such expected liberalization seems defensible including the structural adjustments of economies, so-called just wars, and even "regime change."

But the usefulness thesis of origins with its presumption of the natural liberty of the people has been a ruinous fallacy. It cannot be forgotten that free peoples are entirely the result of their own frenetic practices. This book has been a small effort in political recollection. Absolutely no aspect of free life is latent or lying about waiting to be picked up and better secured in law and other institutions. As is often said, freedom does not come cheap. Hence the usefulness thesis of origins with its offhand references to natural or intuitive liberty resembles, were Cicero here to judge, a great "fraud."[2] Or, assuming no malice is involved in its promotion, the cause of "natural liberty" is a dangerous delusion, for it ignores the tremendous effort needed to produce protofreedom and to have that particular history dominate a society. By (romantically) relying upon "facts" of nature or "human intuition" to supply protofreedom, the usefulness account of origins does not disclose crucial information about half of the investment needed for free peoples. To reiterate, the origins of free peoples are synecdoche producing protofreedom and indictment producing antifreedom, all working continuously, even frenetically. Therefore, the presumed natural or latent liberty of an unfree peoples will never fully blossom if the practice of synecdoche was never underway in their society. And fatefully, even the free peoples will not originate again tomorrow if they do not continue to work hard to maintain themselves along the lines that have been outlined thus far; nature will provide them no aid gratis in that respect.

At some point, the inevitable but sincere attempt at rebuttal will arise, "but is not the liberty of the people valuable or useful?" The answer depends upon the *in situ* deployment of the origins of free peoples. If it appears useful or in their "interests" for a people to revolt or to otherwise better secure their liberty, that is only because they were already considered somewhat free thanks to the enormous and specialized societal efforts made to simulate protofreedom. Curiously, this conclusion sounds like a restatement of Edmund Burke's classic insight that the English people were ready for a "revolution" that secured political liberty because of their "ancient" constitution but not the French people.[3] Although Burke focused primarily upon prior laws, customs, and political institutions, that evidence of a long tradition of promotion of liberty is not in disagreement with the idea that a free people must be familiarized with liberty through synecdochal demonstrations that repeatedly project their freedom back into their history in school lessons, speeches, media reports, in national celebrations and displays, and in philosophical discussions and dissent.

But if the great Irish conservative celebrates the importance of protofreedom for the origins of free peoples, Burke does not equivalently acknowledge the imperative of antifreedom and the practice of indictment employed to refine it. On the latter point, no less crucial for their origins, Burke precisely took issue with "Dr. Price" who had the radical idea that kings were but "servants of the people" and could be "cashiered" by them should they become a threat.[4] Like Kant before him, and liberal thinkers since, Burke either could not or would not address the imperative of antifreedom for the furtherance of free peoples (even though, as a student of

English political history, Burke knew that the development of "the rights of Englishmen" was never a smooth, linear process but a fitful series of struggles). Today, in an age informed by Foucault, Kristeva, and other postmodern theorists, with their concepts of discipline, Panopticonism, abjection, "totalization," and the essential relation with the "other," the harsh construction of difference in the service of politics is not unfamiliar.[5] The terms employed thus far, such as indictment and antifreedom, reflect a more narrow application of those concepts. For Burke, such ideas expressed publicly would be considered unmannerly.[6] But for those who get caught up in the imperative process of indictment, literally sacrificed to the cause, the experience will be far worse than unmannerly.

To consider the fate of free peoples is to raise the question of where their fascination will lead them, not where they will lead others. If the paradigm of charting the future is choice and making the smartest decision, the paradigm of fate is tragedy, which at most bears the option of delaying the inevitable. That free peoples have a fate or destiny is not to belittle their liberty but to fundamentally affirm it. Free peoples are defined by the adoption of freedom as their paramount value, by their fascination with it, or by high liberty. In contrast to what the free peoples themselves might believe they have no choice about their selection of primary value, (otherwise they would not be the free peoples but some other sort of people perhaps the equal, the just, the happy, etc.). In her study of revolution, Arendt applauds the American Revolution over the French Revolution precisely because of the narrow focus of the former upon only liberty. Where the French revolutionaries attempted to secure not only liberty but base "necessity" as well (e.g., the alleviation of poverty), the American founders came close to the ideal achievement of "public liberty" in which an active citizenry debates decisively on the political stage.[7] At the end of the day, notes Arendt regretfully, the ratification of the constitution depoliticized American citizens by having them elect a few representatives to do the public's business.[8] But the nearly successful development of American liberty earns Arendt's praise compared to what she sees in the French experience as the misguided and distracted effort to install *liberté*, *egalité*, plus *fraternité*. Ironically however, the fate of free peoples may ultimately resemble the French experience rather than the American one.

Hyperliberty or real liberty, then, or perhaps some inscrutable combination thereof, seal the fate of the free peoples. Hyperliberty, like Baudrillard's concept of hyperreality, means to insist forcefully on a single principle of political value in the face of overwhelming evidence of other political values.[9] In contrast, real liberty is the expansion of the fascinated, even obsessed, politics of high liberty to include other important values such as equality, justice, or fairness as equivalents. Like the fate of real liberty, the fate of hyperliberty is not to be traced back to any particular policy decision or combination of causal factors. Rather, in terms of origins or as a matter of the particular productive practices imperative for free peoples, their emergence depends upon what Lyotard once called "intensities" or upon precisely how frenetic are the actions taken for high liberty. Metaphorically speaking, hyperliberty is a shout rather than a chant, a fluorescence rather than a glow. Practically, it is additional synecdoche producing more protofreedom and additional indictment producing more antifreedom. The practical meaning of hyperliberty has been anticipated, or was perhaps simply well expressed, in contemporary political theory with the idea of neorepublican liberty.[10] This unsafe variant in the political thought of free peoples deepens their commitment to liberty by increasing the scope of indictment. Where classic liberal theory would identify a current, physical threat to free peoples such as King James II, King George III, or psychopathy, subscribers to hyperliberty also identify "potential" threats to freedom or antifreedom to come.[11] As Boesche puts it, the neorepublican "ideal of freedom does not simply wish to eliminate actual interference but to remove all possible or potential interference."[12] Neorepublican liberty (dubbed neoRoman by Skinner) was rejected when it was proposed in eighteenth-century England in favor of Lockean liberalism because of its legal impracticality (not to mention its vehemence).[13] But the idea has since made a comeback. If however free peoples are already inherently prone to worry about a threatening world around them, then the "freedom as nondomination" of neorepublicanism condemns its subscribers to be wary of threats to come.[14] Like the "precrime" police from the movie *Minority Report*, political and military institutions based upon such a premise will act "pre-emptively" against the probability of threats (thus confirming, if anything could, the productiveness of the practice of indictment identified in this book).[15]

The other possible fate or alternative of note is called "real freedom" (or better, realistic freedom) and represents something of the opposite condition of intensity from hyperliberty. It is a lessening of the acute energies devoted only to the origins of free peoples and their modest diversion instead to other kinds of effects and therefore to other types of peoples. Some free people today, mainly libertarians, recognize the meaning of this change, arguing recently, for example, that universal medical insurance coverage in the United States means the alien arrival of the European social welfare model (i.e., the prioritizing of other political values besides only liberty) on American shores.

Real freedom is the term coined by Van Parij and is the "radical sugges-tion" that freedom cannot be maximally useful unless everyone in society, even the most disadvantaged, is able to maximize their individual liberty. Thus, "one is really free, as opposed to just formally free, to the extent that one possesses the means, not just the right, to do whatever one might want to do." (Van Parij, *Real Freedom for All*, 33). Van Parij nearly exceeds in detail the discussion of threats addressed in Chapter 4 of the *Origins of Free Peoples*. But where the threats to Benn's or Swanton's freedom were various "deficiencies" or "flaws," the threat for Van Parij is that which takes advantage of the real freedom of others and ranges from Marxian exploi-tation to Lockean exploitation to Roemer's exploitation to problems of loafers, cheaters, and free riders. Every version of such exploitation (e.g., capitalist exploitation, loaferism, etc.) illustrates that real freedom is useful by contrast. Van Parij then proposes an "unconditional" national income for all citizens as security for their real freedom against the vagaries of exploitation.[16]

Real Freedom for All is framed as a thoroughly researched and phil-osophically justified policy proposal, but it can also be read as a thoughtful intimation of the fate of free peoples. To an American audience, especially for a libertarian reader, the idea represents the dilution of high liberty and some movement toward high equality. In terms of its intensity, it is a reduc-tion of the energies devoted to protofreedom and antifreedom and diverted instead toward the imperatives of equality or justice. With its array of threats of exploitation including economic exploitation, the idea of real freedom expands the usual process of indictment to include what might be called antiequality and antijustice. To be sure, as Nancy has noted, the value of equality always "belongs" to freedom anyway and cannot be divorced from any political idea of freedom.[17] For example, that every individual is due equal treatment politically is axiomatic for Hobbes, Locke, and today, for every registered voter and democratic citizen. But the standing of equality in much of the modern thought of liberty has always been as a buttress or support for its politics. One fights for equality in free societies only to the extent that the argument can made that one is fighting for freedom. What *Real Freedom* anticipates, however, ever so slightly, is the possibility of a people transformed to promote a multiplicity of paramount values.[18]

When projecting the fate of the free peoples it is important to question their intensity, in this case, by asking whether their liberty will entail more or less effort and "energy" than has typically been devoted to the origins of free peoples. The politics of hyperliberty finds its explicit theoretical jus-tification in the political theory of neorepublican liberty which eschews even the future possibility of domination. Meanwhile, the politics of real freedom have been justified philosophically by the argument for whole freedom or for having the real means, not just the right, to what one wills. But in terms of origins, these rather new politics entail the redirection, increase, or the reduction of the energies traditionally devoted to free peoples and high liberty. The theoretical implications of the "energies" of politics were first systematically considered in Bataille's *Accursed Share*. In Volume 1, Bataille examined historical cases of extreme expenditure or "squandering" from Aztec sacrifice to the Marshall plan and concluded that the contemporary United States should immediately transfer all of its massive wealth to the poor of India in order to avoid catastrophe.[19] His point was that societies are driven not by rationally maximizing utility or profit but by accumulation and then colossal expenditure, preferably in growth or in generosity but often in war. For a Bataille, hyperliberty today, with its endless, "long war" against shadowy threats, reflects precisely the kind of unprofitable waste of gathered resources that he called the "accursed share." Baudrillard's *America*, with its three predictions of either hysteresis (or inertia), metastasis (or overproliferation), or menopause (or conservation) follows Bataille's basic premises.[20] What is helpful about considering the fate of free peoples in this manner is that their origins as synecdoche and indictment are held constant. The only variable is how frenetically their origins are pursued. Hyperliberty or real freedom express and reflect different emphases on that continuum of intensity. In terms of their origins, hyperliberty manifests an increase in indictment or in seeking out anti-freedom. Real freedom manifests a decrease in emphasis upon proto-freedom in favor of other values like equality or justice as equivalent.

If there has been an exogenous factor that has impacted upon the fate of free peoples today, it may be the controversial communications revolution of globalization.[21] Hyperliberty and real freedom might be viewed as responses to globalization. Along with the substantial transfers of information, the transfer of new immigrants (that Huntington identified as a threat to identity) is part and parcel of this new system of pure transmission. In every respect, whether what is exchanged are various ideas or various peoples, what these infinite transfers do to free peoples is dethrone high liberty. To use Baudrillard's metaphors, they make its value "weightless" and force it into "orbit" in order to "circulate" alongside the innumerable other ideas and occurrences that come with globalization.[22] Its communications revolution means that all values then become "virtual," and occasionally "viral," with none any more stable than any other. For Baudrillard, globalization can lead to a kind of ennui on the part of those affected. On this reading, free peoples could respond by simply acting out their customary roles not out of any deep commitment to protofreedom nor from any deep animus against antifreedom but out of inertia from the lack of a clear replacement. Or they might exhaust themselves even more frenetically.

But globalization as pure transmission only begs the question of the fate of free peoples. Given the focus of this study, globalization serves mainly as an illustrative backdrop for the ongoing challenge of maintaining the purity of free society and its fascination with freedom as parmount. If Baudrillard's model of pure communication is contrasted against the origins of free peoples, hyperliberty appears as a kind of forceful reaction against its kaleidoscopic impacts while real freedom reflects an opening to its impressions. From the perspective of their origins however, globalization is not impacting upon free peoples but is being allowed to do so, consciously or not. If so, the decision that is left to free peoples in this political life of their own making is between hyperliberty and real freedom. The former possibility retains their traditional identity as free people, albeit more frenetically, while the latter propels them toward a more diffused, complicated, and joyful type. Alternatively, free peoples may take up both trajectories simultaneously, embarking on a fateful path indeed, for what defined the paradigmatic hero of ancient tragedy was that all anticipated outcomes were ultimately fulfilled.

Notes

1. Zakaria, *Future*, 17.
2. Cicero, *On Obligations*, 104.
3. Burke, *Reflections*, 43, 67.
4. Ibid., 42.
5. Foucault, *Discipline*; Caro, "Levinas," 680.
6. Burke, *Reflections*, 93.
7. Arendt, *On Revolution*, 108.
8. Ibid., 256.
9. Baudrillard, *Perfect*, 22.
10. See Pettit, *Republicanism*.
11. Boesche, "Thinking," 863.
12. Ibid., 862.
13. Skinner, *Liberty*, 97.
14. Hence Costa's call for civility to be added to the harsh, neorepublican model. Costa, "Neo-republicanism," 414.
15. This movie is also cited in Zizek, "The Loop," 206.

16. Only a relatively low "basic income" can be offered or the whole scheme explodes because too many become jealous of the loafers, cheaters, etc. and leap away from this welfare state in what Van Parij (226) calls the "Penguin's Island" scenario. Real freedom has a delicate "equilibrium" point that can be upset by either too much of a threat or too much provision of income. As Van Parij (27) puts it, "[a] free society is one in which people's opportunities are being leximinned subject to the protection of their formal freedom."

17. Nancy, *Experience*, 168.

18. Such future "freedom," critiquing continually and creating variously (and so no longer, on my definition, a free people) is the promising vision of Kioupkiolis, "Three Paradigms," 486.

19. Bataille, *Accursed*, 20.

20. Baudrillard, *America*, 115.

21. Brown, *Politics*, 10.

22. Baudrillard, *Transparency*, 4, 31.

Bibliography

Adler, Mortimer. *The Idea of Freedom*. New York: Doubleday, 1958.

Aeschines. *Aeschines*. Trans. Charles Adams. Cambridge: Harvard University Press, 1919, I: 178.

Appleby, Joyce, Lynn Hunt, and Margaret Jacob. *Telling the Truth about History*. New York: Norton, 1994.

Arendt, Hanna. *On Revolution*. New York: Viking Press, 1962.

Arneil, Barbara. *John Locke and America: The Defense of English Colonialism*. Oxford: Clarendon, 1996.

Ashcraft, Richard. *Locke's Two Treatises of Government*. New York: Unwin, 1987.

—. *Revolutionary Politics and Locke's Two Treatises*. Berkeley: University of California Press, 1986.

Astell, Mary. *Political Writings*. Cambridge: Cambridge University Press, 1996.

—. *The First English Feminist: Selections*. Ed. Bridget Hill. Aldershot, Hants. (UK): Gower Publishing, 1986.

—. *A Serious Proposal to the Ladies*. New York: Source Book Press, 1970.

Barry, Brian. *Theories of Justice*. Berkeley: University of California Press, 1989.

Bartelson, Jens. *A Genealogy of Sovereignty*. Cambridge: Cambridge, 1995.

Bataille, Georges. *The Accursed Share*. Vol. 1, *Consumption*. Trans. Robert Hurley. New York: Zone Books, 1988.

Baudrillard, Jean. "The Ideological Consumption of Needs." *The Consumption Reader*. Eds David Clarke, Marcus Doel, and Kate Housiaux. New York: Routledge, 2003, 255–59.

—. *The Perfect Crime*. Trans. Chris Turner. New York: Verso, 1996.

—. *The Transparency of Evil*. New York: Verso, 1993.

—. *America*. Trans. Chris Turner. New York: Verso, 1989.

Bauman, Zygmunt. *Freedom*. Milton Keynes (UK): Open University Press, 1988.

Beardsworth, Richard. *Derrida and the Political*. New York: Routledge, 1996.

Beddard, Robert. "The Unexpected Whig Revolution of 1688." *The Revolutions of 1688*. Oxford: Clarendon, 1991.

Benn, Stanley. *A Theory of Freedom*. Cambridge: Cambridge University Press, 1988.

Berlin, Isaiah. "Two Concepts of Liberty." *Philosophy: Basic Readings*. Ed. Nigel Warburton. New York: Routledge, 2005, 232–42.

—. Introduction to *Considerations on France* by Joseph de Maistre. Ed. Richard Lebrun. New York: Cambridge, 1994, i–xxxiii.

—. "Joseph de Maistre and the Origins of Fascism." *Crooked Timber of Humanity*. New York: Vintage, 1992, 91–174.

Bodin, Jean. *The Six Books of a Commonweale*. Oxford: Blackwell, 1955.

Boesche, Roger, "Thinking about freedom: review essay." *Political Theory* 26 (1998): 855–73.

Bohun, Edmund. *A Defence of Sir Robert Filmer, Against the Mistakes and Misrepresentations of Algernon Sidney*. London: W. Kettilby, 1684.

Bourne, Henry. *The Life of John Locke*. Aalen: Scientia-Verl, 1969.

Brecht, Arnold. "Liberty and Truth: The Responsibility of Science." *Nomos IV: Liberty*. Ed. Carl Friedrich. New York: Atherton, 1962.

Brenkert, George. *Political Freedom*. New York: Routledge, 1991.

Brown, Wendy. *Politics out of History*. Princeton: Princeton University Press, 2001.

—. *States of Injury: Power and Freedom in Late Modernity*. Princeton: Princeton University Press, 1995.

Burgess, Glenn. *Absolute Monarchy and the Stuart Constitution*. New Haven: Yale University Press, 1996.

Burke, Edmund. *Reflections on the Revolution in France by Edmund Burke and the Rights of Man by Thomas Paine*. Garden City, New York: Doubleday, 1973.

Butler, Judith. "Restaging the Universal: Hegemony and the Limits of Formalism." *Contingency, Hegemony, Universality: Contemporary Dialogues on the Left*. Judith Butler, Ernesto Laclau, and Slavoj Zizek. London, New York: Verso, 2000, 11–44.

Calvert, Randall. *Models of Imperfect Information in Politics: Harwood Fundamentals of Applied Economics*. London: Routledge, 2001.

Caro, Jason. "Levinas and the Palestinians." *Philosophy & Social Criticism* 35 (2009): 671–84.

—. "Looking over your shoulder: the onlookers of Hegel's phenomenology." *Political Studies* 45 (1997): 914–27.

Ciaranelli, Fabio. "The Circle of Origins." *Reinterpreting the Political: Continental Philosophy and Political Theory*. Ed. Lars Langsdorf. Albany: State University of New York Press, 1998.

Cicero. *On Obligations*. Trans. P. G. Walsh. New York: Oxford University Press, 2000.

Clinton, William. "Statement on Signing the Iraq Liberation Act of 1998." *Administration of William J. Clinton, 1998*. Washington DC: United States Government Printing Office, October 31, 1998.

Cole, Douglas. "The Principle of Function." *The Pluralist Theory of the State: Selected Writings of G. D. H. Cole, J. N. Figgis, and H. J. Laski*. Ed. Paul Hirst. New York: Routledge, 1989, 60–67.

—. "The Social Theory." *The Pluralist Theory of the State: Selected Writings of G. D. H. Cole, J. N. Figgis, and H. J. Laski*. Ed. Paul Hirst. New York: Routledge, 1989, 51–114.

Connolly, William. *Identity/Difference: Democratic Negotiations of Political Paradox*. Ithaca: Cornell University Press, 1991.

—. "Identity and Difference in Liberalism." *Liberalism and the Good*. New York: Routledge, 1990.

—. Connolly, William E. *Politics and Ambiguity*. Madison, Wis.: University of Wisconsin Press, 1987.

—. *The Terms of Political Discourse*. Oxford: M. Robertson, 1983.

Connor, W. Robert. *Thucydides*. Princeton: Princeton University Press, 1984.

Consigny, Scott. "Nietzsche's Reading of the Sophists." *Rhetoric Review* 13 (1994): 5–26.

Constant, Benjamin. *Political Writings*. New York: Cambridge University Press, 1988.

Coole, Diana. "Constructing and deconstructing liberty: a feminist and post-structuralist analysis." *Political Studies* 51 (1993): 83–95.

Costa, M. "Neo-republicanism, freedom as non-domination, and citizen virtue." *Politics, Philosophy and Economics* 8 (2009): 401–19.

Cragg, Gerald. *Freedom and Authority: A Study of English Thought in the Early Seventeenth Century*. Philadelphia: Westminster Press, 1975.

Cruickshanks, Eveline. *Glorious Revolution*. London: Blackwell, 2000.

Daly, James. *Sir Robert Filmer and English Political Thought*. Toronto: University of Toronto Press, 1979.

—. "The idea of absolute monarchy in seventeenth-century England." *The Historical Journal* 21 (1978): 227–50.

Davis, Richard. Introduction to *The Origins of Modern Freedom in the West*. Stanford: Stanford University Press, 1995.

Davis, Susan "Checking in the mirror: liberty weekend's patriotic spectacle." *Journal of American Culture* 19 (1996): 61–70.

De Beauvoir, Simone. *The Ethics of Ambiguity*. Trans. Bernard Frechtman. Secaucus, New Jersey: Citadel Press, 1980.

De Maistre, Joseph. *Considerations on France*. Ed. Richard Lebrun. Cambridge: Cambridge University Press, 1994.

—. "De l'état de nature." *Oeuvres Completes* (Paris: E. Vi-te, 1894–1931).

Derrida, Jacques. "Declarations of independence." *New Political Science* 15 (1986): 7–15.

—. *Of Grammatology*. Trans. Gayatri Spivak. Baltimore: Johns Hopkins University Press, 1976.

Descartes, René. *Meditations on First Philosophy*. Notre Dame: University of Notre Dame Press, 1990.

Dillon, Michael. *Politics of Security*. New York: Routledge, 1996.

Donohue, Kathleen. *Freedom from Want: American Liberalism and the Idea of the Consumer.* Baltimore: Johns Hopkins University Press, 2003.

Downs, Anthony. *An Economic Theory of Democracy.* New York: Harper, 1957.

Drake, Paul, and Mathew McCubbins. "The Origins of Liberty." *Origins of Liberty.* Eds. Paul Drake and Mathew McCubbins. Princeton: Princeton University Press, 1998, 1–12.

Dye, Thomas, L. Gibson, and Clay Robison. *Politics in America.* Englewood Cliffs, New Jersey: Prentice Hall, 2001.

Feinberg, Joel. *Rights, Justice and the Bonds of Liberty.* Princeton: Princeton University Press, 1980.

Figgis, John. *The Divine Right of Kings.* Gloucester: Kegan Paul Smith, 1914.

Filmer, Sir Robert. *Patriarcha and Other Writings.* Ed. John Sommerville. Cambridge: Cambridge University Press, 1991.

—. *Patriarcha and Other Political Works of Robert Filmer.* Ed. Peter Laslett. Oxford: Oxford University, 1949.

Flathman, Richard. *The Philosophy and Politics of Freedom.* Chicago: University of Chicago Press, 1987.

Foucault, Michel. *Discipline and Punish.* New York: Vintage, 1979.

—. *The Foucault Reader.* Ed. Peter Rabinow. New York: Pantheon Books, 1984.

—. *Politics, Philosophy, Culture: Interviews and Other Writings, 1977–1984.* Trans. Alan Sheridan, et al. New York: Routledge, 1988.

Fowler, Robert, and Jeffrey Orenstein. *Contemporary Issues in Political Theory.* New York: Praeger, 1985.

Freeden, Michael. *Rights.* Buckingham: Open University Press, 1991.

Fromm, Eric. *Escape from Freedom.* New York: Rinehart and Company, 1941.

Fukuyama, Francis. *The End of History and the Last Man.* New York: Free Press, 1992.

Gallie, William. "Essentially contested concepts." *Proceedings of the Aristotelian Society* 56 (1955/56): 167–98.

Galloway, Joseph. *A Reply to an Address to the Author of a Pamphlet entitled "A Candid Examination of the Mutual Claims of Great Britain and her Colonies," Etc.* New York: James Riverton, 1776.

Garrard, Graeme. "Joseph De Maistre's civilization and its discontents." *Journal of the History of Ideas* 57 (1996): 429–46.

Germino, Dante. *Machiavelli to Marx: Modern Western Political Thought.* Chicago: University of Chicago Press, 1979.

Gobetti, Daniela. *Private and Public: Individuals, Households, and Body Politic in Locke and Hutcheson.* New York: Routledge, 1992.

Gottschalk, Louis. "French parlements and judicial review." *The Journal of the History of Ideas* (1944): 105–12.

Gough, J. "James Tyrrell, Whig historian and friend of John Locke." *The Historical Journal* 19 (1976): 581–610.

Grant, Ruth. *John Locke's Liberalism.* Chicago: University of Chicago Press, 1987.

Gray, John. *Liberalism*. Minneapolis: University of Minnesota Press, 1995.

—. *Postliberalism*. New York: Routledge, 1993.

—. "On liberty, liberalism and essential contestability." *British Journal of Political Science* 8 (1978): 376–90.

Gray, Tim. *Freedom*. Atlantic Highlands, New Jersey: Humanities Press International, 1991.

Haksar, V. "Responsibility." *Proceedings of the Aristotelian Society*. Supplement 40 (1966): 187–212.

Hansen, Michael. "DNA bill of rights; activists call for standards on inmate testing, evidence preservation." *American Bar Association Journal* 86 (2000): 22–28.

Harding, Alan. "Political liberty in the Middle Ages." *Speculum* 55 (1980): 423–43.

Harris, Timothy. "Lives, Liberties and Estates: Rhetorics of Liberty in the Reign of Charles II." *The Politics of Religion in Restoration England*. Eds. Timothy Harris, Paul Seaward, and Mark Goldie. Oxford, Oxford University Press, 1990, 217–41.

Hayek, Friedrich. *Law, Legislation and Liberty*. Vol. 1, *Rules and Order*. Chicago: University of Chicago Press, 1973.

Heideking, Jurgen. "The Image of an English Enemy during the American Revolution." *Enemy Images in American History*. Eds. Ragnhild Fiebig-von Hase and Ursula Lehmkuhl. Oxford, Berghahn Book, 1997, 91–108.

Hibbert, Christopher. *The Roots of Evil*. Boston, Minerva, 1963.

Hill, Bridget. Introduction to *The First English Feminist*. Ed. Bridget Hill. Aldershot: Gower, 1986.

Himmelfarb. Gertrude. *On Looking into the Abyss*. New York: Knopf, 1994.

Hoad, Terry. *The Concise Oxford Dictionary of English Etymology*. Oxford: Oxford University Press, 1986.

Hobbes, Thomas. *De Cive*. Oxford: Clarendon, 1983.

Holmes, Stephen. *The Anatomy of Antiliberalism*. Cambridge: Harvard University Press, 1993.

Honig, Bonnie. "Declarations of independence: Arendt and Derrida on the problem of founding a republic." *American Political Science Review* 85 (1991): 97–114.

Hudson, Grover. *Essential Introductory Linguistics*. Cambridge, Massachusetts: Blackwell, 2000.

Huntington, Samuel. *Who are we?: The Challenges to America's National Identity*. New York: Simon & Schuster, 2004.

Ivison, Duncan. *Political Argument and the Arts of Government*. Ithaca: Cornell University Press, 1997.

James I. *The Political Works of James I*. Ed. Charles McIlwain. Cambridge: Harvard University Press, 1916.

Jones, James. "Revolution in Context." *Liberty Secured? Britain before and after 1688*. Stanford: Stanford University Press, 1992.

Kant, Immanuel. *Religion within the Limits of Reason Alone.* Trans. Theodore Greene and Hoyt Hudson. New York: Harper, 1960.

Kennedy, David. "Culture Wars." *Enemy Images in American History.* Eds. Ragnhild Fiebig-von Hase and Ursula Lehmkuhl. Oxford, Berghahn Book, 1997, 339–60.

Kenyon, John. *The Stuart Constitution, 1603–1688: Documents and Commentary.* Ed. John Kenyon. New York: Cambridge University Press, 1986.

King, John. *Milton and Religious Controversy: Satire and Polemic in Paradise Lost.* New York: Cambridge University Press, 2000.

Kioupkiolis, Alexandros. "Three paradigms of modern freedom." *European Journal of Political Theory* 8 (2009): 473–91.

Klossowski, Pierre. *Sade my Neighbor.* London: Quartet, 1992.

Kojeve, Alexandre. *Introduction to the Reading of Hegel: Lectures on the Phenomenology of Spirit.* Ed. Allan Bloom. Trans. James Nichols. Ithaca, New York: Cornell University Press, 1980.

Krieger, Leonard. "Stages in the History of Political Freedom." *Nomos IV: Liberty.* Ed. Carl Friedrich. New York: Atherton, 1962.

Kristjannson, Kristjan. *Social Freedom: The Responsibility View.* New York: Cambridge University Press, 1996.

Lakoff, George. *Whose Freedom? The Battle over America's Most Important Idea.* New York: Farrar, Straus and Giroux, 2006.

Laski, Harold. "The Foundations of Sovereignty and Other Essays." *The Pluralist Theory of the State: Selected Writings of G. D. H. Cole, J. N. Figgis, and H. J. Laski.* Ed. Paul Hirst. New York: Routledge, 1989, 114–32.

—. *Political Thought in England from Locke to Bentham.* New York: Holt and Company, 1920.

—. *Studies in the Problem of Sovereignty.* New Haven: Yale University Press, 1917.

Laslett, Peter. Introduction to *Two Treatises of Government* by John Locke. Cambridge: Cambridge University Press, 1988, 1–127.

Lazar, Annita, and Michelle Lazar. "The discourse of the new world order: 'out-casting' the double face of threat." *Discourse & Society* 15 (2004): 223–42.

Liddell, Henry, and Robert Scott. *Liddell and Scott's English–Greek Lexicon.* Oxford: Oxford University Press, 1996.

Lipset, Seymour, "Some social requisites of democracy: economic development and political legitimacy." *American Political Science Review* 53 (1959): 69–105.

Lister, Andrew. "Marriage and misogyny: the place of Mary Astell in the history of political thought." *The History of Political Thought* 25 (2004): 44–72.

Locke, John. *Two Treatises of Government.* Ed. Peter Laslett. Cambridge: Cambridge University Press, 1988.

—. *The Educational Writings.* Ed. James Axtell. Cambridge: Cambridge University Press, 1968.

MacCallum, Gerald. "Negative and positive freedom." *Philosophical Review* 76 (1967): 312–34.

McCloskey, Henry. "A Critique of the Ideals of Liberty." *Mind* 74 (1965): 480–94.

MacIntyre, Alasdair. "The essential contestability of some social concepts." *Ethics* 84 (1973): 1–9.

Mackinnon, James. *A History of Modern Liberty*. New York: Longman, Green and Company, 1906.

Maitland, Frederic and Sir Frederick Pollock. *The History of English Law before the Time of Edward I*. Boston: Little, Brown and Company, 1952.

Mansfield, Harvey. "On the Political Character of Property in Locke." *Powers, Possessions, and Freedom*. Toronto: University of Toronto Press, 1979.

Marcuse, Herbert. *Essay on Liberation*. Boston: Beacon Press, 1969.

Mehta, Uday. *The Anxiety of Freedom: Imagination and Individuality in Locke's Political Thought*. Ithaca: Cornell University Press, 1992.

Mendus, Susan. Introduction to *Justifying Toleration*. Ed. Susan Mendus. Cambridge: Cambridge University Press, 1988.

Mill, John Stuart. *On Liberty*. Cambridge: Cambridge University Press, 1982.

Miller, David. "Constraints on freedom." *Ethics* 94 (1983/4): 75–95.

Moore, Barrington. *Social Origins of Dictatorship and Democracy*. Boston: Beacon, 1966.

Nancy, Jean. *The Experience of Freedom*. Stanford: Stanford University Press, 1991.

Nederman, Cary. "Introduction: Discourses and Contexts of Tolerance in Medieval Europe." *Beyond the Persecuting Society: Religious Toleration before the Enlightenment*. Eds. John Laursen and Cary Nederman. Philadelphia: University of Pennsylvania Press, 1998, 13–24.

—. "Principles of Liberty in John of Salisbury." *Difference and dissent : theories of toleration in medieval and early modern Europe*. Eds. Cary J. Nederman and John Christian Laursen. Lanham, Maryland: Rowman & Littlefield, 1996.

Neocleous, Mark. "Security, Liberty and the Myth of Balance: Towards a Critique of Security Politics." *Contemporary Political Theory* 6 (2007): 131–49.

Nietzsche, Friedrich. *Twilight of the Idols and the Anti-Christ*. Trans. R. J. Hollingdale. New York: Penguin Books, 1990.

—. *Untimely Meditations*. Trans. Reginald Hollingdale. Cambridge: Cambridge University Press, 1983.

—. *The Portable Nietzsche*. New York, Penguin, 1982.

—. *The Basic Writings of Nietzsche*. Ed. Walter Kaufman. New York, Modern Library, 1968.

Norman, W. "'Inevitable and unacceptable?' Methodological Rawlsianism in Anglo-American political philosophy." *Political Studies* 46 (1998): 276–94.

North, Douglass, and Barry Weingast. "Constitutions and Commitment: The Evolution of Institutions Governing Public Choice in Seventeenth-Century England." *Origins of Liberty*. Ed. Paul Drake and Mathew McCubbins. Princeton: Princeton University Press, 1998, 17–47.

Oakley, Francis. "The absolute and ordained power of God and king in the sixteenth and seventeenth centuries: philosophy, science, politics, and law." *Journal of the History of Ideas* 59 (1998): 669–90.

Paine, Thomas. "Commonsense." *Political Writings*. Ed. Bruce Kuklick. New York: Cambridge University Press, 1989.

Patterson, Orlando. *Freedom in the History of the West*. New York: Basic Books, 1991.

Perry, Richard, ed. *Sources of Our Liberties: Documentary Origins of Individual Liberties in the United States Constitution and the Bill of Rights*. Chicago: American Bar Foundation, 1978.

Perry, Ruth. "Mary Astell and the feminist critique of possessive individualism." *Eighteenth Century Studies* 23 (1990): 444–57.

Pettit, Philip. *Republicanism: A Theory of Freedom and Government*. New York: Oxford University, 1997.

—. "Freedom as anti-power." *Ethics* 106 (1996): 576–604.

Pitkin, Hannah. "Are freedom and liberty twins?" *Political Theory* 16 (1988): 523–52.

Plowden, Edmund. *The Commentaries, or Reports of Edmund Plowden: containing divers cases upon matters of law, argued and adjudged in the several reigns of King Edward VI., Queen Mary, King and Queen Philip and Mary, and Queen Elizabeth*. London: Brooke, 1816.

Pocock, James. "States, Republics, and Empires: The American Founding in Early Modern Perspective." *Conceptual Change and the Constitution*. Eds. Terrance Ball and James Pocock. Kansas: University of Kansas Press, 1988, 55–77.

—. Introduction to *Burke's Reflections on the Revolution in France*. Indianapolis: Hackett, 1987.

—. *The Ancient Constitution and Feudal Law*. Cambridge: Cambridge University Press, 1957.

Pope, Whitney. *The Search for Freedom*. Columbus, Ohio: Ohio State University Press, 1999.

Prasch, Robert. "Neoliberalism and empire: how are they related?" *Review of Radical Political Economics* 37 (2005): 281–87.

Raphael, David. *Problems of Political Philosophy*. New York: Praeger, 1970.

Rawls, John. *A Theory of Justice*. Cambridge: Belknap, 1971.

Raz, Joseph. *The Morality of Freedom*. Oxford: Clarendon, 1986.

Resnick, David. "Locke and the rejection of the ancient constitution." *Political Theory* 12 (1984): 97–114.

Ricoeur, Paul. *Fallible Man*. Chicago: Regnery, 1965.

Robbins, Caroline. "Algernon Sidney's discourses concerning government: textbook of revolution." *The William and Mary Quarterly*, third series, 4 (1947): 267–96.

Rocquain, Felix. *The Revolutionary Spirit Preceding the French Revolution*. London: S. Sonnenschein & Co., 1894.

Rogowski, Ronald. "Democracy, Capital, Skill, and Country Size Effects of Asset Mobility and Regime Monopoly on the Odds of Democratic Rule." *Origins of Liberty*. Princeton: Princeton University Press, 1998.

Rorty, Richard. *Contingency, Irony and Solidarity.* Cambridge: Cambridge University Press, 1989.

Rosen, F. "Crime, punishment and liberty." *History of Political Thought* 20 (1999): 173–85.

Rudolph, Julia. *Revolution by Degrees: James Tyrrell and Whig Political Thought in the Late Seventeenth Century.* New York: Palgrave, 2002.

Sabine, George. *A History of Political Theory.* New York: Holt, Rinehart and Winston, 1961.

Sallis, John, "Schelling's System of Freedom: Review of *Schellings Abhandlung über das Wesender Menschlichen Freiheit (1809)* by Martin Heidegger" (book review). *Research in Phenomenology* 2 (1972): 155–66.

Sandel, Michael. *Liberalism and the Limits of Justice.* Cambridge: Cambridge University Press, 1982.

Schaefer, David. "Leo Strauss and American democracy: a response to Wood and Holmes." *The Review of Politics* 53 (1991): 187–99.

Schelling, Friedrich. *Philosophical Investigations into the Nature of Human Freedom.* Chicago: Open Court, 1936.

Schmidtz, David and Jason Brennan. *A Brief History of Liberty.* Chichester, U.K.; Malden, Massachusetts: Wiley-Blackwell, 2010.

Schneider, Harold. "The Liberties of Man." *Freedom: Its Meaning.* Ed. Ruth Anshen. New York: Harcourt Brace, 1940.

Schochet, Gordon. *The Authoritarian Family and Political Attitudes in Seventeenth Century England.* New Brunswick: Transaction, 1988.

—. *Patriarchalism in Political Thought.* Oxford: Blackwell, 1975.

—. "Patriarchalism, politics, and mass attitudes in Stuart England." *The Historical Journal* 12 (1969): 413–41.

Schwoerer, Lois. "Locke, Lockean ideas, and the Glorious Revolution." *The Journal of the History of Ideas* 51 (1990): 531–48.

Sen, Amartya. *Inequality Re-examined.* New York: Russell Sage, 1992.

Sidney, Algernon. *Discourses Concerning Government.* Indianapolis: Hackett Publishing, 1990.

—. *The Works of Algernon Sydney.* London: printed by W. Strahan Iun. for T. Becket and Co. and T. Cadell; T. Davies; and T. Evans, 1772.

Simmons, A. *The Lockean Theory of Rights.* Princeton: Princeton University Press, 1992.

—. *On the Edge of Anarchy: Locke, Consent, and the Limits of Society.* Princeton: Princeton University Press, 1993.

Simpson, William, and Martin Jones. *Europe 1783–1914.* New York: Routledge, 2000.

Skinner, Quentin. *Liberty before Liberalism.* New York: Cambridge University Press, 1998.

Smyth, Herbert. *Greek Grammar.* Cambridge: Harvard University Press, 1956.

Sommerville, John. *Royalists and Patriots: Politics and Ideology in England, 1603–1640*. New York: Longman, 1999.

—. "English and European political ideas in the early seventeenth century: revisionism and the case of absolutism." *The Journal of British Studies* 35 (1996): 168–95.

—. *Politics and Ideology in England*. New York: Longman, 1986.

—. "From Suarez to Filmer: A Reappraisal." *The Historical Journal* 25 (1982): 525–40.

Springborg, Patricia. "Mary Astell (1666–1731) critic of Locke." *American Political Science Review* 89 (1995): 621–33.

Swanton, Christine. *Freedom: A Coherence Theory*. Indianapolis: Hackett, 1992.

Tarcov, Nathan. *Locke's Education for Liberty*. Chicago: University of Chicago Press, 1984.

Tarlton, Carl. "A rope of sand: interpreting Locke's 'First Treatise of Government.'" *The Historical Journal* 21 (1978): 43–73.

Thompson, Faith. *Magna Carta: Its Role in the Making of the English Constitution 1300–1629*. New York: Octagon, 1972.

Thucydides. *History of the Peloponnesian War*. Trans. Rex Warner. Baltimore, Maryland: Penguin Books, 1980.

Tuck, Richard. *Natural Rights Theories*. Cambridge: Cambridge, 1979.

Tully, James. *An Approach to Political Philosophy: Locke in Contexts*. Cambridge: Cambridge University Press, 1993.

Tyrrell, James. *Patriarcha non monarcha: The patriarch unmonarch'd*. London: Richard Janeway, 1681.

Van Eeden, Jeanne. "The colonial gaze: imperialism, myths, and South African popular culture." *Design Issues* 20 (2004): 18–33.

Van Parij, Philippe. *Real Freedom for All: What (if anything) can Justify Capitalism?* New York: Oxford University Press, 1995.

Virilio, Paul. *The Information Bomb*. Minneapolis: University of Minnesota Press, 1995.

Von Leyden, Wolfgang. *Hobbes and Locke: The Politics of Freedom and Obligation*. New York: St. Martin's Press, 1982.

Whitehead, Alfred. "Aspects of Freedom." *Freedom: Its Meaning*. New York: Harcourt Brace, 1940, 48–62.

Zakaria, Fareed. *The Future of Freedom: Illiberal Democracy at Home and Abroad*. New York: W. W. Norton, 2003.

Zimring, Franklin, and Gordon Hawkins. *Crime Is not the Problem: Lethal Violence in America*. New York: Oxford University Press, 1997.

Zizek, Slavoj. "The Loop of Freedom." *The Parallax View*. Cambridge, Massachusetts, 2006, 200–51.

—. *The Abyss of Freedom*. Ann Arbor, Michigan: University of Michigan Press, 1997.

INDEX